Reboot America

How the US can Beat China at its own Game

Karan Doshi

Copyright © 2018 Karan Doshi

Dedicated to the Founding Fathers of the United States of
America

The monumental task ahead for Americans today pales in
comparison to what you'll have already achieved

About the Author

Author has a Bachelors and Masters in Chemical engineering. In addition to an interest in his core fields of science and mathematics, he also dabbles in religion, law, politics and economics. He strongly believes that by use of logic and reasoning, one can get the best understanding of the subject at hand and, in many cases, this gives a radically different perspective from the general prevailing trend. He's an avid reader and loves a good debate. He has given talks at college campuses, literary events and has had his articles published in newspapers and other periodicals.

Sign-up to his Mailing list &

get offers on his upcoming Books, invites to his Events and;

get a copy of his first Book 'Land Acquisition in India: Is the farmer wrong?' for Free (in eBook format)

http://eepurl.com/cu_M_D

Visit his Amazon Author Page to shop for all his Books. Check out his pictures, biography and participate in community discussions

http://www.amazon.com/author/karandoshi

Like his Facebook Page and get updates on upcoming Books, Blogs, Events & other promotional offers

http://www.facebook.com/karan.doshi.author

Visit his Homepage for a one-stop summary of all his work

http://www.karan-doshi.com

Visit his Blog to read thought provoking articles on various topics

http://karandoshiblog.blogspot.com

Check out his Goodreads Author page. View his ratings and reviews from the world's biggest site of readers

http://www.goodreads.com/author/show/14825425.Karan_Doshi

Message from the Author

Welcome to my world! I promise an interesting read!

Karan Doshi

author@karan-doshi.com

Bandra West, Mumbai, MH 400050, India

About the Book

The world is changing at a rapid pace. China, the most populous nation on Earth is beginning to assert itself, going from strength to strength on the back of its manufacturing juggernaut. On the other hand, the US, the leader of the free world, is in decline, being saddled with gargantuan debt, stagnant wages and sluggish growth. This Book paints a grim picture of what a future Chinese-led world order would mean, not only for Americans but for us all as world citizens, and cautions against getting carried away by the 'the peaceful rise of China' hype. It further examines the critical policy failures of the US and how China is using unfair trade practices and grand theft of American technology, under the guise of globalization, to pull one of the biggest cons ever. Unlike most other literature on the subject, which typically instills a sense of fear and dread in the reader, concrete suggestions are proffered on how the US can tackle this threat head-on and come back on top.

Table of Contents

I
Introduction

Is America to beware of the Chinese dragon?

I'll be using the word 'dragon' here with every negative connotation of that word to refer to the People's Republic of China. Its meaning will vary depending on context and could refer to the country, the Communist Party, its ideology, its policies, and to a large extent, its people, considering that many Chinese are active supporters of the Party and amongst those who aren't, the majority meekly accept the Party's de facto rule.

The questions are; why has China been labeled a dragon, and why am I cheering for the United States of America, as should be clear from the subtitle.

This Book is about answering that question, although, I'll admit, along a long drawn-out and tortuous path. The quest for an answer will take us through twists and turns, and down winding paths, with each section and sub-section dealing with disparate yet eventually linked ideas, and with logical and reasoned arguments given at each stage to substantiate the conclusions drawn.

Without further ado, let's plunge straight in.

The great unknown of the future; who will emerge as the winner in this rivalry between the US and China? The word 'rivalry' could refer to economic or military rivalry, or in a more general sense, considering that both these countries are vying for the top spot, which country going forward will assume the mantle of world leadership. Will the US maintain its lead or will it cede that position to China?

Of course, there will be some who will disagree with the hypothesis entirely. The reader could instead argue that labeling the healthy free market competition between these two countries as rivalry is taking things too far. Furthermore, considering the carefully worded communiqués released by the diplomats from these two countries, one could indeed be led to think that beyond a few minor issues, there are no real problems between the US and China. After all, they have colossal trade volumes (although this trade is badly skewed in favor of China, which, as will be argued later, should be a significant cause for worry), and are supposedly mutually dependent on each other, and with China holding trillions of dollars of US debt.

However, it cannot be denied that China sees itself as the next emergent power, and if things go per plan, one day will surpass the US [1]. With competition for the top spot and conflicting interests in many areas, one could argue that some form of rivalry is inevitable. Thus, despite China's claims of a 'peaceful rise'[2], many remain unconvinced, and most Americans view China as their No. #1 enemy [8]- so much so that in his election campaign, the 45th President of the US, Donald J. Trump, stated: "We can't continue to allow China to rape our country." [4] Forcing a premature conclusion on the reader, I would have to say that I agree. Of course, I do not expect the reader to necessarily concur with President Trump's or my own views in this matter, but one of the aims of this Book will be to reveal the possible reasons for the President's above aphorism.

The reader may be wondering, why I care. For the record, I am not a US citizen or a Permanent Residence Visa (Green card) holder. I am an Indian citizen. The obvious questions to ask are why I care and why I am taking sides. Why not let these two countries sort it out? The reason is that the winner of this bout will emerge as the next Superpower and will largely shape the future of the world, as we know it. This battle has repercussions for us all as world citizens and not just for the citizens of these two nations.

Considering their opposed ideologies, forms of government and their values, the US and China will not and, rather, cannot share the mantle of global leadership. There has to be a winner. Let me make this clear; the peaceful rise of China, and I have serious doubts about that 'peaceful' part, will signal an end to the US-led world order.

At the outset, I state that I am an Americanophile. I don't know if there is such a word in the dictionary. I know Anglophile is, but as can be inferred, it means that I am a fan of the US. I love its values, the freedoms it has championed, its free and fair legal system, and its government by choice. Overall, I firmly believe that it has been a force of good in the world. Whatever its shortcomings, it represents the best model for creating prosperity for everyone, and a way to guarantee basic freedoms for all. Many around the world, especially those in countries where governments suppress the rights of its citizens, see the US as an inspiration, which, if given a choice, they would love to be a part of. This Book is, therefore, not just about how the US can beat China, but also why it is essential that it does so, not only for the US itself, but also for the rest of the free world.

The reader, of course, need not share in this opinion. Therefore, I have devoted a substantial portion of this Book to develop the basic argument as to the 'why' before the 'how'. Why is it imperative for the US to win this new Cold War. Take note, and as will be continually espoused in this Book, this battle of attrition is indeed a new Cold War. The one thing that is missing is for someone to stand up and say it explicitly, as Churchill once did with his 'Iron Curtain' speech.

Judging by the general negative portrayal in the world media of the US, which is especially true after the recent Trump victory, it would indeed seem that the majority of people around the world have an unfavorable opinion of the US. Reactions have varied from mild aversion to outright hatred. By me, this negative portrayal is strongly biased, and it is high time someone gave the other side of the story.

In addition, I also endeavor to develop some common sense ideas concerning basic economics. These notions will be required later on when it comes to giving concrete suggestions by which the US can best China. Taking a quick detour, let's take the example of the recent mortgage crisis and the resultant meltdown in the global markets due to the insane risks taken by financial experts at the big Banks. It is these very experts who lent to high-risk borrowers viz. the subprime owners, at ridiculously low interest rates, and that, too, on capital borrowed at crazy leverages in the confidence that even if the buyer were to default, the property could be repossessed and auctioned at a higher price. Why? Because, as the argument went, property prices have risen in the past and will continue to do so in the future, thereby eliminating risk. Any rookie will tell you that to assume a market rising in perpetuity is just plain stupid.

Just an example but only when these core economic and political ideas are well established, and I believe it is essential that I do so, will specific suggestions be offered to counter the Chinese threat. Of course, these suggestions are applicable not just to the US but to all countries that value freedoms, democratic institutions, the rule of law, and want to safeguard their way of life and ensure their progress, prosperity, and survival through the ages.

The reader could find many books already written on this topic enumerating the threat from China. This is a well-researched topic with many published books, and is constantly debated ad-nauseam, say, on the TV, blogs, chat forums, YouTube etc. The general trend followed by most authors is to instill a sense of fear and panic amongst the readers, especially amongst their American audience. This Book is different in that not only does it articulate the obvious threat from China, but it also offers concrete suggestions and ideas to tackle and eventually negate it. I believe that this is something of value added here that the reader won't much find elsewhere. To complain and to scare is one thing, but to find ways of solving a problem, quite another. This is the big step forward here.

II
Is there really a problem?

Firstly, I guess, we should ask ourselves if there is such a big problem here. Is the US in terminal decline and is such a dramatic wake-up call, as will be argued in this Book, required. Furthermore, is China such an ascendant power and are the two countries' value systems so vastly different that rivalry and at some stage, probably even conflict, is inevitable.

In short, is there a genuine raison d'être for this Book. Is the situation that bad or is it that the US is going through a rough patch and the other way around for the PRC (People's Republic of China) that one can ride this wave and things will eventually pan out? I will be arguing that the situation is quite serious and won't automatically self-correct, and if it continues this way, there will be a tipping point from which there is no return.

At the very least, it cannot be doubted that China is currently the ascending power and the US is on the ropes. For the naysayers who will point to slowing growth rates in China, it has to be realized that China is also maturing as an economy, and to expect the 15% growth rates as was the case in the 1990's[5] is unrealistic. However, despite this slow down, the growth rate still hovers around 7%[5], which is substantially more than that of the US and many other nations.

At the same time, it cannot be denied that all is not well with the US, especially on the economic front. The recent mortgage crisis is but one example. It later ballooned into one of the biggest Wall Street crashes in history, possibly even bigger than the 1929 crash. To quote the Chairman of the US Federal Reserve, "September and October of 2008 was the worst financial crisis in global history, including the Great Depression"[6].

This slowdown reverberated throughout the world, especially amongst the economics of Western Europe, leading to drastic measures being adopted, such as bailouts in the hundreds of billions of dollars. In some countries, interest rates, the minimum guaranteed interest earned by parking your money in the safest of places, that is with the country's Reserve Bank, were reduced to near zero (negative in Japan).[7]

The spinoff of this economic crisis was a sustained Bull run in Gold. Gold is a contrarian indicator. When markets do well, Gold generally falls or stagnates and vice versa. To explain, imagine you as an individual investor want to grow your wealth. You look out for investment options like lending money to friends or family, investing in a business venture, buying property, putting it in the stock market or even buying art. However, let's say there's an economic downturn and you have no confidence in any of the aforementioned investment avenues. What do you?

Not invest, as it would carry the unnecessary risk of taking a loss. You would rather wait out the storm. You would keep your monies at home under lock and key. On a big picture level, it means investing in Gold. Gold is a safe dependable and ever marketable asset. When everybody does that, the demand for the yellow metal goes up and the price of Gold increases. As simple as that.

Coming back to the economic woes of the US, the most worrying of its problems is the gargantuan amount debt it has amassed. A few figures for reference:

- A vast Federal Debt pegged at 19 trillion dollars

- The total Debt per citizen of more than 200,000 dollars (800,000 dollars per family of four)

- Debt to GDP of 104%

- A Federal budget deficit of around 680 billion dollars

- State Debt of about 1 trillion and Local Debt of close to 2 trillion dollars

- Mortgage Debt resulting from the mortgage crises just shy of 14 trillion dollars

- Total personal Debt of 17 trillion dollars and

- Spiraling Social Security and Healthcare liability of 16 and 27 trillion dollars respectively

- Total US Govt. Debt of 65 trillion dollars

All this combined with personal debt totaling to liabilities of a 101 trillion dollars.[8] Further compounding the problem and relevant to our discussion is the trade deficit with China that stands at some 365 billion dollars annually.[9]

At first glance, it would indeed seem like game over for the US, and many would argue that the US couldn't come out of its debt trap. I wouldn't want to speculate, but it cannot be denied that this enormous debt should be a significant cause for worry.

The problem is further exacerbated by the US's inability to control spending. This is due to two reasons; one, of course, is massive spending by the government, even compared to many other Western countries of comparable lifestyle and development, on healthcare and social security.[10] Just these two make up a considerable portion of the debt. The other reason, as will be argued later, is an inability of the US to generate wealth by investing in industry and infrastructure. Thus, despite this massive spending by the government, precious little of value is being created with regards to improved infrastructure or better quality of life. In fact, the general perception is that the infrastructure in the US today is worse now than ever.[11] On a private level too, the average American citizen seems to be spending more than they are earning, considering the total personal debt of around 18 trillion dollars in total or about 200,000 dollars per capita.[8]

The main problem, as will be argued, is that the US has stopped creating wealth, the one sure-fire ticket to posterity. I will be arguing that the chief reason for this is a near total outsourcing of its industry and manufacturing to China. All the wealth that manufacturing once created is gone. This has led to a classic situation of spending more while at the same time closing off avenues of earning or generating wealth. This double whammy does not portend well for America's economic future. Some will say that outsourcing is a good thing as prices have gone down because of cheaper manufacturing in China. Many will insist that this is the ultimate realization of Globalization. America is 'evolving' into a service-based economy from a manufacturing one, which is the supposed next stage in the US's growth story. I couldn't disagree more, but let's leave this debate for later.

Let's come to China, the other side of the proverbial coin. At the very start, the US having an annual trade deficit of 365 billion with China would mean equivalently that China has a trade surplus of the same amount with the US.[9]

Further statistics for reference with regards the Chinese economy:

- Astronomical levels of Forex (foreign exchange) reserves of around 3 trillion dollars[12]

- GDP which has grown exponentially in the past thirty years with rates averaging 10%[13]

- Current GDP of 14 trillion (Nominal) and of 25 trillion dollars (Power Purchasing parity) beating even that of the US (at PPP)[13]

- As is common knowledge, China has become a manufacturing hub having the largest manufacturing base anywhere in the world[18]

- It is the largest exporter in the world[18]

- It has the world's fastest-growing consumer market[18]

- China is also the largest trading nation in the world with many countries having China as their largest trading partner, replacing the US that historically held that position.[18]

- China has also gone for Large-scale Industrialization and development of Infrastructure and Housing on a level unseen anytime in human history with factories manufacturing almost every conceivable product and supplying it not only to local markets but around the world. It has undertaken massive spending on infrastructure in building of new roads, railways, airports, power generation plants and of modern cities with high rises to house the millions of its burgeoning middle class.

Take note of the Chinese Premier, Xi Jinping's dream of achieving the 'Two 100's': The material goal of China becoming a 'moderately well-off society' by 2021, the 100th anniversary of the Chinese Communist Party, and the modernization goal of China becoming a fully developed nation by 2049, the 100th anniversary of the founding of the People's Republic.[18] Such is the confidence that the Chinese have in their future and justifiably so. I would indeed agree that modern day China is well on its way to achieving these goals.

The contrast couldn't be starker.

One country is ascendant while the other descendant. The financial figures are like mirror images of each other. If one has a surplus, the other has a deficit. If one is a manufacturing hub, the other is being increasingly made devoid of industry. It is interesting to note that until some time ago industry was seen as the backbone of economic strength. Images of development, prosperity and economic power had interspersed in their background images of large-scale industries with the rack-pinion, the spanner tool, the conveyor belt and factories with tall chimneys and such. Nowadays, what goes for the symbols of wealth are images of Wall Street, the dollar sign, the trading floor, the zigzag stock price graph going up and won but invariably rising upwards and other symbols not associated with industry but more with trading and marketing of securities and other fancy financial products. Somewhere down the road, these trading symbols have replaced those of industry in our collective imaginations as the future driver of economic growth. Those who disagree, and count me amongst the detractors, are taken to be old-fashioned and out of touch with the times.

Markets are the driver of economic growth, or so the experts proclaim. I won't deny their benefits in toto, but here's the crux. Facts on the ground somehow don't seem to support this hypothesis. The champion of the market economy, the United States, is in decline, and the poster boy of industry, China is going from strength to strength. Strange, isn't it? Something seems to have gone wrong here.

Only once we admit to something being amiss can we proceed to analyze what exactly has gone wrong and from then on come up with ways to fix it. Therefore, I firmly believe that there is a genuine reason for this Book.

Many authors stop at this first stage of showing that something is badly wrong, and, I daresay, they do it rather well. However, I want to take it further by examining the broad issues that ill the current economic system, which will help us to come up with a solution. I do not believe in scaremongering and instilling a sense of pessimism in the reader. Let's admit the problem, examine and study its underlying causes and then try to fix it.

First, though, I want to take a slight detour and impress upon the reader, whether American or a citizen of any other country in the world (possibly including China) as to why the rise of China is a serious threat and why a US-led world order is infinitely superior to a Chinese led one.

III
Why I love the US...

Even if it has been established that China is winning and the US is in decline, the obvious question to ask is why the reader (especially the non-US citizens amongst you'll) should care. For that matter, why should I? I owe no citizenship obligation to the US.

In this and the next chapter, I will try to convey my reasons for the same. Why am I an Americanophile and why do I fear and at times downright tremble at the thought of a Chinese-led world order. Referring to the subtitle of the Book on how the US can beat China, I strongly believe it is imperative to first justify the 'why'. The next couple of chapters focus on this.

I don't have hard statistics to prove this point, but nowadays there is a general trend of portraying the US in a bad light. It ranges from an outright visceral hatred of the United States to maybe at least an undertone of negativity. Whether it is in the news media, social forums or even at private dinner parties, whenever any topic on international events crops up, someone will start with the usual US bashing, blaming it for many of the ills of the world.

I couldn't disagree more. One of the common recurrent themes to throw mud at the US is Bush's ill-fated invasion of Iraq, the standard charge being that the invasion was a pretense to steal Iraqi oil. That what Bush claimed about Iraq's weapons of mass destruction (WMDs), which admittedly were never found, was not a genuine intelligence failure but a purposeful lie told to justify Iraq's invasion and subsequent oil theft. Admittedly, the US finds itself on the back foot here, but I would like to give a quick rebuttal, if it's not straying too much from the topic at hand.

- I believe Bush did not invade Iraq for its oil, as it is nigh impossible to 'steal' oil. It would require an immense investment of resources and time to extract oil from the ground and ship it clandestinely out of the country. One cannot set up an entire industry of extraction and processing overnight, especially in a country with near nonexistent supporting infrastructure crippled by years of prior sanctions.

- Iraq is earning today close to 46 billion dollars annually from its oil exports.[14] To put it simply, when the US is paying for it, it cannot be called theft.

- The US spent 2 trillion dollars on the second Gulf War.[15] That's around 10 times its annual oil import bill of 10 million barrels per day x $58 per barrel x 365 days/year = 210 billion dollars.[16] Thus, even if the US were to steal its entire oil demand from a fledgling, read nonexistent, Iraqi oil industry, it would take ten years of stealing just to make up for its War costs.

- Bush genuinely and, in hindsight, mistakenly believed Saddam had WMD. Take note that Saddam had used WMDs as far back as 1988 when he bombed Halabja with mustard gas that killed over 5,000 Iraqi Kurds.[17] The assumption that if Saddam had it then, he would have it now, is quite a natural one to make.

- Let's be honest, weren't we all surprised when no WMDs turned up. Why would Saddam keep stalling those UN inspectors for more than ten years if he had nothing to hide? After all, this game of cat and mouse cost him his seat of power, his grand lifestyle and eventually even his life. Why indulge in such a high stakes game when you can just allow the inspectors in, who would report that they didn't find any WMD, and the entire casus belli for an invasion falls through? Was Saddam mad not to allow the inspectors in especially when Bush had given him a final ultimatum and, especially so, when he had nothing to hide? I find it hard to get my head around his stupidity.

- Even if Saddam had no WMD, is it that bad if Bush took steps, even if, in hindsight, it were for the wrong reasons, to eliminate a brutal Dictator who meted out unspeakable horrors of mass killings, use of chemical agents, torture, rape and theft on his own people? Even if removed for the wrong reasons, is it not one more step taken by humankind in its quest to rid the world of old antiquated ideas of absolute dictatorships and give the

Iraqi people an opportunity to form a representative government of their own choosing?

Thus, I state this with utmost candor of what I believe Bush's real thinking was for the invasion of Iraq. For him, post 9/11, the only way to put an end to Islamic terrorism would be to sow the seeds of democracy in the Middle East. All of the countries of the Arabic speaking Middle East have some sort of a dictatorship, whether it is a religious theocracy or hereditary monarchy or plain military dictatorship. Saddam was probably the worst of the lot. To cross him being an Iraqi in Iraq would've been suicide. The people of Iraq would, quite plainly, not have had the guts to rise in insurrection. The invasion of Iraq was an attempt by Bush not to seize oil but to remove Saddam and establish a working democracy, which, according to him at least, would have acted as a beacon for the rest of the Middle East. It was hoped that the seeds of democracy would spread all across and pave the way for the democratization of the entire Middle East, leading to secular governments, having rule of law, governments working for the betterment of the people rather than dictators enriching themselves and wherein the youth are gainfully employed. This would have dealt a body blow to terrorism. At least that was Bush's thinking. The opposite and rather simplistic and popular, but at the same time naive argument is that it was all for oil. Take your pick.

I encourage the reader to see the other side of the coin when it comes to the Iraq War and not get carried away by that one-sided notion of oil theft. Even today, for example, Iraq cannot extract enough oil to satisfy US demand, forget covering the costs of the War. Think about that. I spend a

1,000 dollars on trying to steal a 100. Doesn't make sense, does it?

Some readers might accuse me of being an unabashed fan of the US, obfuscating the negative points while glorifying the good. However, the opposite view of America being the root cause of all evil in the world, responsible for all the wars, the unrest and even indirectly responsible for the birth of ISIS[18], is a much more widely preached narrative, without any firm evidence, without any clear reasoning, and many a time, stemming from personal prejudice. Allow me an alternate, and, even if slightly exaggerated, a much-needed perspective on the positive aspects of the US and what it stands for, and for which, I believe all of humanity should be eternally grateful.

Let's go ahead and list some of the positive aspects of the US, something that is missing from the current dialogue and is thrust so far back in our minds that we've pretty much forgotten about them.

The US was the first country, in modern times, to show that there can be a kingdom/country without a King. They defeated the British, the superpower of the day, and instead of establishing a hereditary monarchy with George Washington as their new King, they decided to abolish that institution altogether and make way for an elected representative to temporarily hold the top post.

One could argue that the concept of democracy was also developed in the United Kingdom. Other than Britain, however, the US was the only other country to carry that torch forward in its day. In fact, the rallying cry of the

American Revolution was 'No Taxation without Representation' a clear reference to the demand by the inhabitants of the erstwhile US colonies to have a say in the elected bodies of the UK, a right enjoyed by their British brethren.

The rest of the world at that point pretty much followed the principle of having an absolute Monarch who could rule and do as He pleased, who had the power to suppress dissent and the power of life or death over you, which in many cases He freely exercised, especially so, if you were critical of His rule.

What is surprising is that there are many countries even today, including China for that matter, that do not have the checks and balances of a modern democratic government, but instead have an absolute ruler, either through a one-Party rule or a reigning Monarch or Dictator who has seized power outside of the ballot box. Surprisingly, the world media, which is generally critical of even minor infractions of the US, seems to take this absolute ruler concept in its stride with scant criticism, as in the case of Iraq under Saddam or with regards to China, especially so after Xi Jinping had himself declared as ruler for life[19].

All those who are critical of the US, let us understand that it has been the champion of democracy in the world. If you are able to exercise some form of the right to criticize without fear of persecution, it is because of the spreading of these democratic principles, primarily championed by the US, across the world, including to my own country of India.

I recall an interview of a Mr. Michio Kaku, a Japanese descent American theoretical physicist, on YouTube, who was being constantly heckled by a Russian TV journalist. In the interview, the female journalist was running down the US, its foreign policy, and trying to have Mr. Kaku make critical remarks against the US.[20] At one stage, it was clear that Mr. Kaku got annoyed, and one of his comments stands out. To paraphrase Mr. Kaku; that you want me to criticize the US and admit its wrongs but you forget that I have the right to so criticize because of the democratic ideals allowing for criticism and dissent championed by the US itself. Isn't that the beauty of the US system?

Could the woman journalist, being a Russian citizen, openly criticize her President, Vladimir Putin? Would she suffer pangs of anxiety and fear for life and limb for having a negative and critical view of the Russian President? I bet she would. Russia, under Putin, has also increasingly become an authoritarian State with the opposition systematically sidelined and detractors imprisoned. Putin, like Xi, is looking like another ruler for life.

The US essentially replaced the concept of rule by King to that of rule by law wherein an independent Judiciary decides your case on merits alone, free of fear or favor. You are not subject to the whims and fancies of a King or his prejudiced and controlled inner council.

The two cornerstone documents of the United States are the Declaration of Independence and the Bill of Rights. These are two of the most important and fundamental texts ever penned by the hand of man that define, protect and glorify the dignity of a human being. At some level, they supersede all of the achievements of humankind, and these honorific texts deserve to be given the greatest of importance even, without wanting to get into a debate, superseding religious texts.

To quote the Declaration of Independence: "We hold these truths to be self-evident, that all men are created equal, that they are endowed by their Creator with certain unalienable Rights, that among these are Life, Liberty and the pursuit of Happiness".[21] That the US has mostly lived up to these ideals in securing for its citizens the aforesaid rights for the past 250 odd years is an achievement having scant equal in human history.

To quote some of the statutes from the Bill of Rights[22]:

"Congress shall make no law respecting an establishment of religion, or prohibiting the free exercise thereof; or abridging the freedom of speech, or of the press; or the right of the people peaceably to assemble, and to petition the Government for a redress of grievances." A right, for example, being denied in many Islamic countries wherein Islam is the State religion and the State actively discriminates against minorities. Again, I ask, why is the world media silent on this?

"No person shall be held to answer for a capital, or otherwise infamous crime, unless on a presentment or indictment of a Grand Jury, except in cases arising in the land or naval forces, or in the Militia, when in actual service in time of War or public danger; nor shall any person be subject for the same offence to be twice put in jeopardy of life or limb; nor shall be compelled in any criminal case to be a witness against himself, nor be deprived of life, liberty, or property, without due process of law; nor shall private property be taken for public use, without just compensation."

"In all criminal prosecutions, the accused shall enjoy the right to a speedy and public trial, by an impartial jury of the State and district wherein the crime shall have been committed, which district shall have been previously ascertained by law, and to be informed of the nature and cause of the accusation; to be confronted with the witnesses against him; to have compulsory process for obtaining witnesses in his favor, and to have the Assistance of Counsel for his defense."

"Excessive bail shall not be required, nor excessive fines imposed, nor cruel and unusual punishments inflicted."

Take note that a government of the people, by the people and for the people, wherein the people choose their elected representatives, have a right to change them if they feel otherwise, wherein fundamental rights are guaranteed in perpetuity by a sacrosanct document called the Constitution allowing for a right to dissent and to criticize, which is so crucial in any democracy, is a gift by the US to a world of absolute rulers and dictators or religious zealots wherein human life was otherwise considered cheap.

Of course, in this long walk towards freedom, it cannot be denied that the honors have to be jointly shared with Great Britain and partly with France, but the major contributions made by the US are undeniable.[23]

For example, the French revolutionary war cry of liberty, equality, and fraternity stands as an inspiration for all those aspiring to democratic ideals,[24] though it could be argued that the French may have well taken their cue from their American brethren who had defeated the British and had already set up their own democratic system of government by then.

However, it would be remiss of me not to talk about the role played by Great Britain. From the signing of the Magna Carta to electing their aldermen to counsel, to it being further sanctified by establishing a House of Commons and eventually have this Lower House supersede the traditional power base of the King viz., the House of Lords over the course of many centuries of struggle, to Bills passed guaranteeing the independence of the Judiciary, to universal suffrage for all, including serfs, laborers, and eventually women; yes, a large part of this long march was undertaken jointly by Britain.

It is important to note that pretty much no other country figures in the list. We in India, for example, took our system of government from the British and our Constitution was borrowed, especially the most crucial chapter on fundamental rights, from the Bill of Rights of the US. No other country which is a democracy today is democratic because of its own ideals and values, but are so by having borrowed these ideals from the big two viz., the UK and the US and partly France. Furthermore, of course, there are even today many countries that are monarchies or absolute dictatorships or, like China, have a Communist one-Party rule.

When the French political activist, Alexis de Tocqueville, visited the US in 1831, he was shocked to see that there were no social barriers between the elites and the common folk. The average citizen of the US did not defer to the elite class. A landowner could sit across the table from a carpenter and share a drink. A society wherein, through hard work, it was possible for a commoner to make it rich and live the life of what could be called a minor aristocrat in old-world Europe. To quote de-Tocqueville: "Among a democratic people, where there is no hereditary wealth, every man works to earn a living. Labor is held in honor; the prejudice is not against but in its favor"[25].

In effect, the US freed itself from the shackles of old-world European aristocracy, nobility, and the social class by introducing a government, to quote Lincoln, "of the people, by the people, for the people"[26]. This represents one of the most significant changes in status quo in all of human history. Since time immemorial, there has been a ruling and a privileged class of people who ruled over the underprivileged common folk. That this change was brought about mainly by the US, and successfully at that, stands as one of its most significant contributions to human intellectual progress.

So ingrained are these sentiments of a ruling class prevalent in many parts of the world, that in democratic India even today, the ruling class, which are now elected, still behave as a privileged and entitled lot. Whether it is forcing the common Indian citizen to use the honorific 'Sahib' to refer to them, a title historically reserved for British civil servants. Whether it is stopping traffic to get right of way without planning for any alternates or without any care for the hardships of the people. It's been reported that in some cases, even ambulances have been made to stop. Whether it is having an armada of police who behave rudely and shove people around as if clearing the thoroughfare for royalty, this feeling of entitlement persists even today. In fact, India has one of the lowest police to people ratios in the world, with one policeman for every 720 people,[27] and of these a significant proportion get assigned to this VIP duty.

The United States established the first secular state wherein there is no official State religion. In fact, they put that right there in the Bill of Rights, and I quote: "The civil rights of none shall be abridged on account of religious belief or worship, nor shall any national religion be established, nor shall the full and equal rights of conscience by in any manner, or on any pretext infringed."[28].

Today, freedom of religion is taken for granted in many secular democracies in the world, including in India. We owe this to the US taking the lead. I'm not saying there aren't any religiously motivated hate crimes in the US, but let's understand that they are rare and the State protects the rights of minorities and imposes severe punishments on violators.

Take note that religious freedom was not the norm in the past. Most countries, kingdoms, monarchies, or provinces were ruled with a majority religion having sway over all subjects of all religions and the adherents to that majority faith, in general, got preference and special privileges over minorities. This was accepted as standard practice.

Strangely and sadly, this is true of many countries even today. For example, there are no Hindu temples, Buddhist monasteries or Jewish Synagogues in Saudi Arabia.[29] Furthermore, Saudi Arabia is not the only country to so ban any other form of worship other than the State religion, in this case, being Islam. In fact, many Muslim countries either ban or actively discourage the practice of minority religions. In fact, the word Islamic is appended to the name of many Muslim majority countries, clearly stating their distinct religious preference. There is active discrimination going on even today on the basis of religion in many countries around the world. To do justice to this topic would probably require its own Book. However, I want to ask, why does all of this go on with scant criticism from the world media? Imagine if the US were to rename itself the Christian States of America or ban Mosques. All hell would break loose.

Of course, as stated, there have been incidents of religious hate crimes in the US, but let's understand that those attacks are on a personal level; the government and the law is not actively involved in discrimination. That the Christian right exists in the US is not denied, but by and large, it is within the limits of advocating its faith without restoring to hate crimes or using force or coercion to convert. As I said, the day the Christian right renames America and bans other religions is the day I will criticize it and that too not before I criticize other nations that are doing it as on today. As an aside, this list indirectly also includes China, which frowns upon all forms of religious worship altogether.

Criticism which is one sided is worse than no criticism at all. Hardly an eyebrow is raised for the clear and open discrimination against minorities in the Islamic world. Here's a maxim: Thou shalt not criticize the US if at the same time and before that thou have not criticized the far more repressive religious policies in other countries. Be fair.

Saudi Arabia was recently elected chair to the United Nations Commission on Women's Rights. Talk about a more inappropriate candidate for the job, a country known for its gender-biased laws, where women cannot even leave their house without a male escort.[30] It's sad but at the same time, I find it somewhat funny. I mean, how can the UN do this? To reiterate, there is so much wrong going on in this world on which critics are all silent, but some little thing about the US crops up...

For those who are lamenting the supposed erosion of religious freedoms today in the US and point to an attempt by Trump to ban Muslim immigration; let's get things in perspective. Firstly, let's understand that the granting of visas is a privilege and not a right. The US reserves the right to invite to its soil whomsoever it pleases. It goes without saying that whoever is so privileged to be so invited should demonstrate a respect for that country's laws and values.

Let's talk about the countries of the Middle East. Most, probably all, of them are Muslim majority States. Almost none of them allow for any immigration. As a non-Muslim, the chance of me becoming a permanent resident or citizen of these countries is essentially zero. No protests regarding this? No claiming this is unfair. Trump has tried to curb Tourist Visas but allows for legal immigration of Muslims into the US. On the other hand, there is no way for a non-Muslim to become a citizen of any of these countries in the Middle East.

I recall a news item, post the Trump Visa ban, which depicted a scene in which people were offering Muslim prayers (Namaz) at US airports as a sign of protest. Consider this; if I were to offer my Hindu prayers in public (I am Hindu-Jain) in a Muslim majority country, say, Saudi Arabia, I would be beheaded.

The media sees the travel ban imposed by Trump on citizens of some high-risk Muslim countries. Note again that Trump allows for Muslims who are on non-tourist visas to one day become permanent residents and eventually citizens. The media does not publicize and censure the total and complete ban by the Middle East countries on immigration especially of non-Muslims and their policies of active discrimination against minorities. Why?

Getting China into the picture, something overdue as this Book is on that, it's no secret that it has limited tolerance to the practice of any religion. For example, Falun Gong practitioners are considered a national security threat by the CCP (Chinese Communist Party). As a brief primer, Falun Gong is a form of spiritual practice of self-improvement through meditation and some form of exercise like body stretches.[81] It's not even a full-fledged religion. However, many Falun Gong practitioners have been arrested and thrown into labor camps, reminiscent of Soviet era Gulags, for the 'crime' of practicing this 'religion'. In addition, many Tibetan Buddhists, Muslim Uyghurs and Catholics face imprisonment, harassment and even torture at the hands of the CCP.[32] No sound bite in the media on this?

Moral: I will not criticize a student who gets an A for not getting an A+ while at the same time letting a student with a D- off without a reprimand.

The next big contribution of the United States has been in the path towards scientific enlightenment. That America has contributed massively to the advancement of the scientific spirit is undeniable.

What is true, and how can truth be established? Is something true because I tell you it is so, your near and dear ones tell you so, you read it in a religious book, or you hear of it from an elder in your community? This was is not a foolproof way of establishing truth. It stands to reason that truth can be determined by fact-checking. Propose a theory to explain whatever it is that you want explained, conduct an experiment and collect data. Then compare the predictions of your theory with the experimental data. If they match consistently and repeatedly, you can say with confidence that what you have theorized is right and conclude based on that. Till then, and this is important, without fear or shame, feel free to admit your ignorance.

This is, in essence, the scientific method. The Oxford Dictionaries Online defines 'the scientific method' as "a method of procedure that has characterized natural science since the 17th century, consisting in systematic observation, measurement, and experiment, and the formulation, testing, and modification of hypotheses"[33].

Though many would vehemently disagree, this remains the best and the only method of arriving at truth. What is written in a religious text can be wrong, what your trusted friend tells you may be incorrect, what your gut feeling tells you may be inaccurate. However, when evidence is obtained for something by conducting multiple experiments, each yielding the same result time and again, common sense and basic reasoning should force you to accept the conclusion, whether you like it or not. That's the beauty of repeated experimentation. It eliminates personal bias, heresay or coincidence.

Acceptance and encouragement of the scientific spirit has resulted in genuine theories that have helped us understand the underlying laws that govern our Universe, from the smallest atom to the formation of galaxies. The contribution that Americans have made in this endeavor is undeniable. By understanding the laws and then putting them to good use, we have made human existence much more comfortable, providing us with inventions like the light bulb, the airplane, the car, long distance communication, life-saving drugs, etc.

This same logic carries forth to the Law. A Judge pronounces a verdict after weighing in the evidence. You need evidence to convict. Personal beliefs, gut instincts, prejudices don't count.

By separating religion from State affairs, as was alluded to earlier, the US not only established a secular state but also gave scientific inquiry a free rein. By encouraging a questioning attitude and providing funding and recognition to scientists and academia, the US has largely shaped the scientific and technological revolution of our times.

I do not deny that scientific progress started in Europe during the Renaissance with greats like Kepler, Galileo, and Newton or even in earlier times in ancient Greece by the likes of Pythagoras, Euclid, and Archimedes. The Greek period ended, most would agree, with the murder of Hypatia and the burning of the library of Alexandria by religious zealots, plunging the world into what is called the Dark Ages. European scientific progress for the longest time faced a hostile Church and was dependent on the largesse of the rich and fickle nobility for funding and patronage. It was in the US where scientists were seen more than just court jesters, were freed from religious persecution and a serious effort made at funding them. This included salaries and terms that afforded scientists financial security to carry out their work without having to worry about routine matters of, to say it crudely, putting food on the table.

Do a count and you'll notice that the largest numbers of Nobel Prize winners are American. From the simple light bulb to life-saving drugs to the car, the airplane, and the telephone, these scientific and technological inventions have changed our world.

Furthermore, as alluded to earlier, the US is the true champion of establishing the world's first secular state wherein the State is independent of religion. When the Declaration of Independence was being drafted, the words 'We hold these truths to be self-evident, that all men are created equal...' were of the form "We hold these truths to be sacred and undeniable, that all men are created equal..."

It is to the everlasting credit of the founding fathers that they removed the word sacred, an indirect reference to God or religion and replaced it with rationalism, implying that by virtue of logic and reasoning we can arrive at the truth of equality for all.[84]

The scientific equivalent of the same, though not overtly stated but tacitly assumed, is that the 'truth' of how the world or the universe works or of any phenomenon big or small can be ascertained by logic, reasoning and experiment rather than by blindly accepting whatever is written in a religious tome. The most famous example would be the geocentric hypothesis of the Earth being the center of our Solar system and also of the Universe as is stated in Christian Scripture most vociferously propounded by the Roman Catholic Church to the extent of having Galileo put under house arrest until death for holding a contra heliocentric and, needless to say, correct view.[85]

That Science has answered so many questions that were in centuries past attributed to divine intervention, and further by use of that knowledge has vastly improved our lives and given us near superhuman powers, has abundantly validated that approach and has changed our lives in unimagined ways. Few people who hate the US would bat an eyelid before using the car, an airplane, a television, a mobile phone, a light bulb, medicines etc. These are mainly American inventions. I could go on, but one telling statistic is that America has 353 Nobel Prize winners while my country of India, having close to four times the population, has 10.[86] Anything special about Americans; are they a superior people? Well, I wouldn't say that. It is that the US provides scientists and inventors a free rein; free in all respects, be it politically, socially, scientifically, and most importantly, from religious persecution. Furthermore, by giving their scientists financial security in terms of research funds, salaries, teaching posts at universities and, if successful, the right to patent their inventions and have a chance to monetarily benefit, the US has become a Mecca (with apologies for the religious reference) for scientists.

The US then used this acquired scientific knowledge to fuel a massive Industrial Revolution. Through the use of basic Science, one gets to understand Nature better. One can then use that knowledge to ones advantage. That's the technology part of the science and technology equation. It is the practical applications of what is conjectured by theory and established as truth by experiment.

The Industrial Revolution has forever transformed our lives in ways unimagined. Imagine telling someone from four hundred years in the past that you have in your hand a device by which you can talk to anyone anywhere on this planet, that you could see on some glass screen events from around the world, or you could travel by flying to anyplace in the world under 24 hours goings at speeds in excess of 800 km/hr. They'll think you're crazy. Crazy at first, but if you were to demonstrate it, he'd think you were God. Our entire modern day existence is based on pure scientific discovery followed by the technological invention of devices, gadgets, and equipments mass-produced in factories. Manufacturing is so ubiquitous today that we almost take it for granted that if we want some product, there must be a factory somewhere making it.

Granted, the Industrial Revolution did not start in the US, the honor for this going to Great Britain. However, there is one key difference between the US and the UK in this regard that I'd like to point out.

One big positive aspect of US industrialization as opposed to the industrial economies of Europe is that the US did not pursue colonies that would act as ready markets for its goods. The British needed their colonies as a source of cheap raw materials and as a market for their finished goods, India being the jewel in the crown of this Machiavellian scheme of how one country got rich at the expense of the other. The accepted zeitgeist of that time was that this was a good thing as the 'natives' of the colonized lands were considered inferior and the white man was, in fact, doing a favor on the supposed grateful natives as industrialization got prosperity for all, even if it was badly skewed in favor of the Colonial powers. It was considered the 'white man's burden' to 'civilize India' and to bring the rule of law to these colonized lands suffering from centuries of historical barbarian rule under despotic Monarchs.[37]

To quote the words of Jules Ferry, twice Prime Minister of France, "In the area of economics, I am placing before you, with the support of some statistics, the considerations that justify the policy of colonial expansion, as seen from the perspective of a need, felt more and more urgently by the industrialized population of Europe and especially the people of our rich and hardworking country of France: the need for outlets {for exports}... I repeat that the superior races have a right because they have a duty. They have the duty to civilize the inferior races..."[88]. I dare say economic theory at that time considered it almost impossible to have the growth of one nation without some form of subjugation of another. The argument was, where else other than in those colonized lands do we find a cheap source of raw materials for our factories and a ready market for our finished goods wherein we enjoy a near monopoly, especially so, since we've have banned local factories?

The US stands as a prime example of why this type of thinking is wrong. Kudos to the US that it could develop to become one of the top industrialized nations in the world without having to subjugate other nations, getting rich by merely using in-house raw materials and a market comprising its own citizens. In one fell swoop, it threw centuries' worth of economic dogma out of the window and proved that one man, predominantly of a white disposition need not get rich at the expense of another, predominantly of a brown or black disposition.

One could argue that slave labor constituted a de facto colony of sorts and thus the US is no angel in this regard. I cannot deny that slavery existed and represents, probably, the most brutal form of human repression and as many could argue, was worse even than colonization. Yes, point well taken. However, let's understand that by the 1850s there was already a recognition in the US that slavery was evil and an attempt was made, and a successful one at that, to abolish it. The American nation took a big risk by taking this stand, risking its existence by fighting and eventually winning a Civil War that threatened to rend the country in two. Furthermore, it is interesting to note that the bulk of the development in industry, manufacturing or economic growth in the US occurred in the decades following the Thirteenth Amendment to the US Constitution abolishing slavery.[39]

Few people realize that after the World Wars, especially the Second one, the US could easily have held on to the territories that it had 'liberated'. It could have held onto France, Spain, Italy, Belgium, Netherlands and the Western half of Germany, not to mention Japan. Most battles throughout history have been fought this way where the conqueror kept his conquered lands. In fact, the Soviet Union did just that, holding forcibly onto the countries of Eastern Europe, by suppressing with tanks the Hungarian uprising and building a Wall to keep its subjugated citizens in. Again, to the eternal credit and the magnanimity of the US, it liberated Western Europe in the truest sense of the word and, in fact, spent its own money through the Marshall Plan to get their economies, devastated by War, back on track. That it later formed NATO is a given, but it was a willing alliance of willing partners.

Alternatively, imagine what the world would be like if Germany or Japan had won the War. That the Japanese thought themselves to be superior to other Asians is obvious by their utter disregard for human life as is well documented by the horrible atrocities meted on the conquered peoples of Asia. Similarly, Germany had its Nazi ideology of a superior Aryan race who thought of themselves to be the rightful inheritors of this planet. This led to their extermination of the Jews, whom they considered inferior, and their dreams of Lebensraum, which is a forced expulsion of the local populations of Eastern Europe to make way for German settlers.

That development without subjugation is possible was proved by the US, which applied this formula so successfully that it eventually rose above all of the colonial powers of Europe. This, again, is a huge contribution made by the US towards promotion of basic human rights and dignity. When it could easily have done so much wrong, it did so much right.

Coming to the present time, this manufacturing base that lead to prosperity in earlier years has taken a back seat in the US today. Factories have been shifted out, and the mantle of industrial leadership has been handed over to China. Whether this is a cause of worry is the central question this Book attempts to answer.

To recap, we as citizens of this planet owe a big debt of gratitude to the US for shaping, to a large extent, what's best in our societies today in almost all fields: politics, economics, scientific thought, form of government, basic human rights, guarantor of free thought, the right of dissent and freedom of worship. That the US is not perfect is a given, but for a country barely 250 years old, especially so when compared to other societies and civilizations that have been around, some for thousands of years, this is indeed a remarkable achievement. Let's all take a bow.

IV
Why my animosity towards China…

The People's Republic of China is in many ways an antithesis of the US. Thus, the reasons as enumerated in the previous chapter of why I love the US could be turned around into reasons of why I dislike the PRC.

For starters, China is a Communist Dictatorship, dissenters and detractors beware. No democracy, no vote and no choice. The Communist Party has existed for the past 60+ years and plans to go on doing so forever. If you like the system, well and good, but if you don't, that's your problem. The all-powerful Party promotes a blind and unquestioning acceptance of its authority. It's just the way the communist system works.

The CCP seems to have borrowed a leaf from the ancient Chinese tradition of having an Emperor, revered almost as a God.[40] Needless to say, the Emperor hardly ever lived up to that ideal, many a time being so isolated from his subjects, locked up in the Forbidden Palace, that he had little knowledge or care for the issues at hand.

To take a slight detour, most Eastern traditions have this concept of absolute obedience to their elders. Obeying your parents unconditionally and without question was considered a virtue, and this concept carried forth to the common folk taking those in authority, for example, the Emperor, as a kind of a father figure or demigod requiring unconditional obedience. I am not saying that children should continually disobey or bicker with their parents, but on the other hand, this unquestioning mindset dulls the intellect. Personally, I advocate a healthy questioning attitude towards those in authority.

To give a quick summary of the clear negatives of the model as adopted by China:

- A Communist Dictatorship at the helm of with no hope for any alternate form of government

- A non-independent Judiciary that is subject to the Communist Party's diktat

- Limited to nonexistent fundamental rights, chief amongst them being the right to criticize and of dissent

- Establishment of a privileged class of Party members, wherein this elite have been known to flout the rules for personal benefit, leading to large-scale corruption

- Lack of religious freedoms

The reader can easily assess how this system in many ways represents a contrast to the one followed in the US.

However, taking a contra stand, it can be argued that despite its shortcomings, the Communist Party has worked wonders for China. I wouldn't be writing this Book otherwise.

Under the leadership of the Party, China has seen explosive growth in the past three decades with per capita income having grown from around a 100 dollars in the 1970s to 8,000 in 2017.[41] That China is an ascendant power can hardly be denied with its massive industrial base and its growing economic and military clout in the world. When compared to other democratic and developing nations like India, which got its independence in 1947 vis-à-vis the Chinese, wherein the Communist Party came to power in 1949, it is clear that China has far surpassed India in many areas, especially in per capita income, which is almost five times greater.[41]

A comparison between India and China will start a new debate that I want to avoid here. Though I will mention one important aspect that often tends to be overlooked, which is that though India was a democracy, it was so only in a political sense. Economically, it was anything but free with economic reforms beginning only in 1991, post the fall of the Berlin Wall and the dismantling of the former Soviet Union. This opening up subsequently led to much higher growth rates and an increase in prosperity. China remained communist in a political sense only having its one-Party rule and denying individual freedoms, but economically it emulated the western capitalist system of free enterprise and competition after the opening up of its economy in 1979, post Nixon's visit.

After the death of Mao Zedong in 1976, his successor Deng Xiaoping is said to have proclaimed something to the effect that getting rich is not a bad thing.[42] Consider that it is these economic freedoms that made China leap forward to its current position today while India stagnated under socialist and inefficient State-run monopolies. Thus, it could be argued that though India was a democracy, it was so only in the political sense and was economically shackled. China, post 1979 remained politically closed but from that point on economically open.

Thus, the CCP, the Chinese Communist Party, should be named more appropriately, though somewhat blandly, the 'Politically Communist but Economically Capitalist (one-way) Party of China. The addition of the word 'one-way' is significant and will be taken up later. Let it be understood that China was indeed hard-core communist, both economically and politically, till the death of Mao. From then on, however, it started emulating the capitalist model and thus paradoxically owes its success to an economic policy championed by the US.

It would, therefore, be reasonable to ask what would have become of China without the guiding beacon of the US free market system. Today we see the growth phase of China, but what of its past? China was not the poster child of development in those days. When I talk of my animosity towards China, it partly stems from the hellish life of ordinary Chinese citizens in the first half of the CCP's rule. The excesses committed by the Communist Party in propagating its misguided goal of creating a socialist utopia and the untold hardships suffered by millions of its subjects cannot be ignored. This is and will always be a problem with a totalitarian system. When they work, they can do well, but when they follow misguided policies with no check and balances, it can create hell on earth. It is surprising how few people know of China's disturbing experiments with socialism and fewer still that are raising the alarm.

Let's get to the first of Communist China's two big socialist 'experiments' before the opening of its economy.

THE GREAT LEAP FORWARD

Or, the way I prefer to call it, the largest mass scale starvation event in all of human history. Officially, this was an economic and social program of the Communist Party from 1958 to 1962. The negative repercussions of this misguided policy were such that it led to the removal of Mao Zedong, the patriarch of Communist China. That he plotted his return in the Cultural Revolution is a story for later.

The main aim of the Great Leap Forward was to rapidly modernize China through a massive collectivization and industrialization drive. All private ownership, especially farm ownership, was banned, and all farms were made part of a socialist 'collective' wherein the farmers toiled for land that belonged to the State. Many were worked to exhaustion. Those who objected were branded as counter-revolutionaries and brutally punished.

As is typical of an incompetent bureaucracy, the State promulgated flawed agricultural practices, set unrealistic yield targets and with corrupt officials siphoning off funds, there was in fact a decline in overall crop yield. What made a bad situation worse was when Mao dictated that the country simultaneously embark on a massive industrialization drive, specifically with emphasis on the production of iron and steel, and that too at the village level. Rather than set up large-scale factories with high-end technology to produce quality steel, it was decreed that each village would take up the challenge by setting its own local unit. Thus, each village erected its own crude blast furnace with limited technological knowledge. The quality of steel so produced was mediocre and of no real value. So carried away were the people by this propaganda that in many cases, they threw existing and well-made iron and steel products like pots and pans and door handles into the furnace in an attempt to boost production. Imagine the stupidity of it all. Throw ready and quality steel in a blast furnace to make crude, lousy, low quality steel.

Worse was to come. In their fervor to make steel, farm hands were diverted to the effort with the result that nobody bothered to sow or harvest that year's crop. The result was large scale famine. No quality iron or steel ever got made, and as there was no one planting the crop, there was no food harvested. Mass scale starvation set in. People were reduced to scavenging for whatever they could find with horror stories of people cooking the dead to feed the living.[43]

This resulted in an estimated death toll of around 30 to 55 million people.[44] That's like nine times the number of Jews murdered (approximately 6 million) in the Holocaust.[45] That human life was considered so worthless by the Communist Party can be gauged by Mao's adage: "When there is not enough to eat, people starve to death. It is better to let half the people die so that others can eat their fill"[46]. Imagine the cruel, crude logic of the Party that showed no remorse for the forced starvation of millions of its own subjects.

Dear readers, that's the Great Leap Forward. Entire volumes can be devoted to its excesses. Not many know about this event in China's relatively recent past. It should serve as a wakeup call. If a State can so turn against its own people in such a barbaric way, what can the rest of the world expect when the Chinese Communist Party is at the helm of world affairs?

Let's move on to the CCP's next big bad idea.

THE CULTURAL REVOLUTION

This is the next trial by death idea of Mao, which he used more like a ploy to claw back to power following his suspension post the Great Leap Forward. The Cultural Revolution lasted 10 years from 1966 to 1976 and is an example of State-sponsored terrorism against its own people. It's estimated that around 36 million people were persecuted, of which around 2 million were killed and roughly the same number permanently disabled. However, other estimates put the death toll at between 5 to 10 million people.[47] The stated goal was to preserve true communist ideology by "purging remnants of capitalist and traditional elements from Chinese society and to re-impose Mao

Zedong Thought as the dominant ideology within the Party".

Squads of Red guards, mostly students, went from town to village punishing anyone they deemed counter-revolutionary. No fair trials, no right of dissent and no respect for individual views was ever accorded. The worst affected were the intellectuals. They were publicly humiliated, arbitrarily imprisoned, tortured, forced into hard labor, endured sustained harassment, had their property seized, and sometimes executed. In many cases, it was reported that students went to schools to round up their own teachers.[47]

In the words of historian Anne F. Thurston, "(the Cultural Revolution) led to the loss of culture, and of spiritual values; loss of hope and ideals; loss of time, truth and of life".[47]

As stated, volumes can be written on the excesses of these two events. In the annals of human history, one will be hard pressed to find events of comparable magnitude and horror as these two.

That a system like this, though partly reformed today by emulating some western ideals, could one day be at the helm of world affairs makes me shudder. Should one ignore this past and move on? That the CCP is much reformed today is given. However, note that this reform has not come around by any internal soul searching but by emulating western ideals. Not that the CCP is even today anywhere close to being a bastion of human rights. If you think it's time to bury the past and move on, I disagree. At the same time, I won't argue this point any further.

Before I move on, a moment of silence. In memory of the millions of Chinese dead...

I now draw your attention to some of the modern day excesses of the CCP.

Let's start with the comparatively minor ones.

I take the case of Anastasia Lin, a Chinese Canadian model. She is a Canadian national having emigrated from China. She won the Miss Canada Title in 2015 and was set to represent Canada in the Miss World 2015 pageant to be held in Hainan, China.[48]

In addition to being a model and an actor, she is also a political activist. She has criticized China's human rights record, especially its treatment of Falun Gong practitioners, something I'll be taking up later in this section. For her views, and unsurprisingly so, she was denied a Visa to participate in the Miss World competition and was declared persona non grata.[48]

Needless to say, and I won't keep repeating this, the reader should take it as implied throughout this chapter that critics would have jumped at this unmerited treatment of Miss Lin if the US had done anything of the sort. Shocking, isn't it, that China could bar a contestant from a reasonably powerful and developed country like Canada and that Canada didn't do much beyond token criticism, and the rest of the world carried on with the pageant? The Miss World organization also turned a blind eye to this forced disqualification and in doing so, I believe, failed to live up to its own maxim of 'beauty with a purpose'.

On a more worrying note, Anastasia Lin's father, who is still living in China, is the target of the CCP. He isn't allowed to leave the country and is being constantly threatened by Chinese security agents. Anastasia has been continuously getting distressing phone calls from him, forced by the authorities, begging her to stop her activism.[48]

Coming to the part of land ownership. It could be argued that the CCP has indeed turned over a new leaf from its communist ideology of the Great Leap Forward and the Cultural Revolution by emulating the West in its economic reforms and, at least from the economic angle, things are definitely better now than they ever were during the 'real' communist times.

However, there is one economic sector in which the CCP still clings to its old communist ideal; land ownership. In China, land is not a private asset that can be held and owned by its citizens. Land belongs to the State, which in this case means the Party. The Chinese don't own their homes; they can only get it on lease from the government. On expiry of that lease, the house reverts to the State. This gives the State enormous power, which, one shouldn't be surprised considering China's record at corruption, is being misused.

The problem arises when the State goes about acquiring land by displacing existing settlers for its infrastructure projects. In principle, I'm not against land acquisition for the greater good such as setting up industries or building infrastructure. However, in China, land acquisition is a harsh process. Land is acquired giving scant notices to those being displaced. It could happen that one day a bulldozer may show up at your gates and ram your house to the ground.

Furthermore, a significant portion of the compensation due ends up with local Party officials. Corruption, as is well known, is endemic in China. This leads to an inability of the displaced to find alternate and equivalent housing, leading to an increase in poverty in the minority displaced even if the project would overall improve the quality of lives of the majority in the end. Thus, even when the CCP tries to do well, such as improving infrastructure by building roads, airports, dams, etc., the slipshod, corrupt and entitled way in which it goes about it leaves much to be desired. This results in a certain section of the people, those whose land is being acquired, feeling cheated and humiliated. There have been reports of beatings, imprisonments and even killings in the process.[49]

Moving on to one of the most brutal and absurd excesses of the CCP that is, the persecution of Falun Gong. Let's understand more about this movement first. Many already know of it but to give you a primer, it was a spiritual movement started by a Mr. Li Hongzhi that promised a betterment of your mental health through a series of exercises similar to the Yoga or Pilates. Furthermore, it advocated living a truthful and compassionate life.[31] That's about it. In all seriousness, I ask, what could possibly be wrong with that?

Somehow, the CCP considers Falun Gong to be a serious threat to its own hold on power. The reader may wonder how precisely a peaceful practice of meditation and yoga type exercises can pose a threat to the authoritarian control of the Chinese Communist Party. Honestly, even I fail to understand this. However, if given to wild speculation, I would say that it was merely because of the movement's popularity.

The Falun Gong movement became exceedingly widespread with adherents inside China alone of around 70 million people.[31] To the Communist Party, which zealously guards its own cult as the sole provider of leadership to the Chinese people, this was seen as a threat. By me, this is plain jealousy taken to an extreme. The Chinese government started a nationwide crackdown in which they arrested Falun Gong practitioners in the hundreds of thousands, imprisoned them without trial, and interred them, not in prisons, but in specially designed labor camps, a concept harking back to the days of the Soviet gulag. Conditions were abominable. Abuses include forced labor, torture, psychiatric abuse and other forms of mental 'reform' in which the Chinese authorities tried to undo the 'damage' done by the Falun Gong philosophy and instill the standard Marxist-Leninist-Maoist thought.

The big fear seems to be that quasi-religious movements are a risk to the power structure of the State and thus Falun Gong is nothing short of a national security threat and its practitioners are traitors to the Party cause. Insiders have called this crackdown a mini Cultural Revolution of sorts. Mini by the standards of the past, but a crackdown in which hundreds of thousands have been arrested and face detention without trial can hardly be called 'mini'.

Of all the atrocities committed against the Falun Gong detainees, and the list is extensive, the worst to my mind is that of organ harvesting. An estimated two hundred thousand Falun Gong members have had compulsory surgeries on them in which their organs were surgically removed, (for example, kidneys and liver) for supply to the organ donor market.

I repeat, as a punishment for being a member of an organization advocating compassion and truthfulness and doing some body stretches to help cope with the stresses of daily life, members of Falun Gong were considered counterrevolutionary, arrested, tortured, forced into concentration camps and had their organs surgically removed. Of course, to state the obvious, one cannot live without your liver or both your kidneys. Thus, this organ harvesting business was necessarily a death sentence.

Governments of Australia, Spain, Israel, the US, Taiwan, and Italy have passed resolutions condemning this practice, and so has the United Nations Committee against Torture.[50] I quote from the US House of Representatives, Resolution 343, that draws attention to the "persistent and credible reports of systematic, state-sanctioned organ harvesting from non-consenting prisoners of conscience in the People's Republic of China"[51]. To quote Representative Ros-Lehtinen "The Chinese regime's brutal repression, and human rights violations, are well-known, but it is the horrific treatment of the Falun Gong practitioners, Mr. Speaker, that is particularly egregious, yet does not receive the attention that it deserves"[51].

In a similar vein, let's continue on to the more general case of the CCP meting out capital punishment. China executes the maximum number of people annually, in fact, more than the rest of the world combined. Could this be because the Chinese are inherently more criminal by nature? I think not. The answer is that the CCP recommends the death penalty for offenses that generally would not attract that punishment in most free societies. As you might have guessed, some of the crimes relate to being engaged in activities subversive not to the State, such as being a traitor to your country by selling military secrets, but instead being a traitor to the official Party line. Criticize the CCP at your own peril. In fact, the CCP would routinely 'order' courts to mete out the death sentence if it feels it necessary to protect its influence and power base. So much for the independence of the Judiciary. Somehow, Falun Gong practitioners fall into this category and so do a disproportionate number of Tibetans and Uyghurs.[52]

China has what at best can be described as a mediocre criminal justice system. Many of the basic tenets of a free and fair Judiciary are absent with prisoners languishing for years in prison without ever seeing the inside of a courtroom or even a formal charge brought against them, something the United Nations has termed "an urgent human rights concern"[53]. What is generally absent is a free and fair trial, basic rules of evidence, the presumption of innocence and punishment commensurate with the crime. Judges can be swayed by local Party officials. To give an example, there was a case reported of a Party official's son who was charged with rape being acquitted and an innocent bystander who tried to help the victim, sentenced.

As was indicated earlier, China, in addition to its regular prisons, has a labor camp system specifically for dissenters and political prisoners. Imagine having a Soviet-style concentration camp system well into the 21st century run by a major world power housing an estimated two hundred thousand inmates. Many are imprisoned, as the reader would've guessed by now, not for any actual crime but for dissenting political or religious views and detained without trial and forced to work as slave labor in mines, factories or farms. Satellite imagery shows enormous complexes rivaling any Soviet gulag or Nazi concentration camp. A few crimes reported are:

Jiang Chengfen, 40, female, a farmer from Sichuan interred for criticizing the government

Guo Qinghua, 46, female interred over an argument with Party officials over her pay. Incidentally, though unsurprisingly, she reports having seen jailed Falun Gong members there.

Ma Liangfu, 54, male, interred for trying to prosecute the sons of some local politician. These sons were trying to rape a girl, and when Ma tried to stop them, they blinded him in one eye. The Court acquitted the politician's sons and, instead, sent Ma to the labor camp.[53]

Let's now get to the plight of Tibetans. To give some historical background, Tibet and Xinjiang were independent territories before the 1950s. The PRC invaded and forcibly annexed them into the Chinese mainland. The Dalia Lama, the Tibetan spiritual leader, was forced into exile, and he fled to India. In essence, Tibet got invaded and occupied overnight without the world raising a finger. Even, India, being Tibet's neighbor and with whom it shared historical cultural and religious links dating back thousands of years, did not respond to the Dalai Lama's pleas for help, other than giving him sanctuary at McLeod Ganj, where he resides today . Tibetans, as many would know, have long since been fleeing Chinese rule by escaping to India through Nepal. The reasons are many, from religious persecution to being treated as second-class citizens in their own land to a Party policy that actively tries to obliterate their culture and way of life.

Recently, the CCP has come up with a novel plan to solve the Tibet issue. Considering that these areas are marginally populated compared to the Chinese 'main' land, the Party has started a systematic procedure of resettling the traditional Han peoples of China proper into Tibet. Such is the population shift that soon the Tibetans will be a minority in their own land. Their aim is to 'Han-ify' Tibet and, also Xinjiang, which has a significant Muslim population. I have to admit, the plan is brilliant in its simplicity. Tomorrow, if ever a plebiscite were held, which is most unlikely, the majority would end up voting to remain in China, considering their original Chinese Han roots. That China will not let go of Tibet is clear, but if by some miracle the Western powers were ever to force a plebiscite, they will be shocked by the result and would then have to accept the majority vote. Brilliant.

As stated, many Tibetans fearing persecution and wanting to continue their way of life have no choice but to escape over the arduous Himalayas into India. The mountain crossing is dangerous with some of the world's tallest peaks with having to battle the terrain and unpredictable weather with minimal modern equipment. However, from now on these escaping Tibetans have to battle one more threat. Chinese soldiers have been ordered to shoot at sight escaping Tibetan refugees. Can you believe that? An order to shoot your own citizens. An incident of a shooting has been recorded as it happened in Nangpa La, and available on YouTube.

That's not all though. As if taking pot shots, with live ammunition, at your own people was not good enough, the Chinese government has decided to go all high tech in this shooting game. The Chinese army has deployed drones to do the dirty work. Imagine these automated drones hovering along the border areas and shooting escaping Tibetan refugees. These drones can go up close and shoot at point blank range and they work night and day. Killing your own citizens and making an industrial scale project of it. Trust the Chinese to do it. [54][55]

Let's turn to Hong Kong. The Chinese Govt. made a pledge to the UK before the handover that it would respect Hong Kong's sovereignty under the one country, two systems formula and that it would not interfere in the democratic process of the territories of Hong Kong. That this would have been an empty promise should have been clear to anyone who has had any experience in dealing with China. Anyway, in a sign of clear meddling, the CCP, through its wing, the NPCSC (Standing Committee of the National People's Congress), issued a decree of proposed reforms to the Hong Kong electoral system. Understand that these reforms were not proposed by the elected members of the Hong Kong Parliament but by mainland CCP. The proposals were repressive and amounted to getting a Chinese OK before any candidate was allowed to contest for a seat in Hong Kong's legislature.

This led to massive protests, mainly by students that later came to be known as the Umbrella Revolution. The Chinese government denounced these peaceful protestors, a right citizens enjoy in any serious democracy, for violating the 'law' and warned them of severe consequences. The Hong Kong government, subservient to their Chinese masters, misused the courts and police powers in an attempt to suppress the Revolution by use of force like baton charges and false arrests, thus forever besmirching the independence of the Hong Kong police and its judiciary. There have been so many instances of the CCP's active meddling in Hong Kong's affairs from deciding who can stand up for election, to getting the CCP's approval for the next leader and the use of courts and police to do its bidding, that it is clear that Hong Kong is no longer a functioning and vibrant democracy. I openly ask this question; was Hong Kong better off under British rule?

Hu Jia, an activist, is quoted as saying, "Two of the world's powerful autocracies, both rooted in the idea and practice of communist dictatorship, are bent on encroaching upon freedom and democracy on two different fronts: Ukraine and Hong Kong"[56].

A few headlines for the reader's perusal:

"Chinese censors are trying to erase Hong Kong's pro-democracy movement."
Quartz[57]

"Hong Kong pro-democracy politicians banned by China as crisis grows."
The Guardian[58]

"As Hong Kong Chooses Its Next Leader, China Still Pulls the Strings"
The New York Times[59]

"Hong Kong court bans pro-independence politicians from office."
The Guardian[60]

"Hong Kong Pro-Democracy Activist Joshua Wong Denied Entry to Thailand"
The Wall Street Journal[61]

"Hong Kong protests: Demonstrators set for backlash as China's strangulation of the Umbrella Revolution begins."
Independent[62]

"China tries to snuff out separatism in Hong Kong."
The Economist[63]

"Legislators challenging China's grip on Hong Kong barred from office."
The Globe and Mail[64]

Let's take the case of Joshua Wong. He is a Hong Kong citizen and an active member of the pro-democracy movement calling for democratic elections to the post of Hong Kong Governor rather than just going with China's pick. A university in Thailand invited him to be a guest speaker to address students on his role in the movement. China was not too happy about this and used its influence on the Thai government to block his speech. He was not even allowed entry into Thailand where, by his account, Thai immigration officers at Bangkok airport blocked his entry and told him he was on a blacklist. He was detained for 12 hours and then flown back to Hong Kong.[65]

"Deporting Hong Kong Umbrella Movement activist 'China's business', Thailand says"
ABC News Online[66]

Wong was later arrested in Hong Kong and sentenced to six months for unlawful assembly during the Umbrella Revolution and also barred from holding public office for five years.[67] So much for one country, two systems.

Until now, we have covered the atrocious way that China punishes its own citizens who deviate from the accepted Party line. Let's get on to instances of how China tries to get to you even if you're not a Chinese citizen and not in China. Disturbingly, there have been cases reported of the long arm of the CCP harassing non-Chinese citizens who are critical of China. I've already given you the example of Anastasia Lin, a Canadian, who was denied entry to the finals of the Miss World contest. Of course, it goes without saying that if you are a Chinese citizen residing in China, it's best to stay within your boundaries as you literally risk life and limb.

Another example, also given, is of Joshua Wong, technically a Hong Kong citizen. Alternatively, take the example of Gui Minhai, a Hong Kong bookseller who disappeared from his home in Thailand and was seen months later in Chinese police custody. His crime; selling books critical of the Chinese regime.[65] Let's take another example: Li Xin, a Chinese journalist, also disappeared from his home in Thailand. One day his wife got a call from him telling her that he had 'willingly' gone to China and was being investigated for some crime, exactly what, he did not specify.

Such is the threat of Chinese bullying that many Chinese citizens in Thailand have sought refugee status from the UN as they fear being kidnapped and whisked away to China with the tacit acceptance of the Thai government which does nothing to prevent what should be a blatant violation of its own sovereignty.[65]

This may surprise the reader, but I refer to the case of an American citizen, Richard Gere,[68] a famous Hollywood actor and human rights activist. He converted to Buddhism on one of his visits to India and is a supporter of the Tibetan cause. He regularly visits the Dalai Lama at Dharamshala, India, the headquarters of the Tibetan government in exile. He is a co-founder of various activist groups supporting the Tibetan cause like the Tibet House, Director of The Gere Foundation and Chairman of the Board of Directors for the International Campaign for Tibet. As can be expected, this has drawn the ire of the CCP. That he is permanently banned from entering China is no surprise. However, the economic clout of the Chinese government extends to Gere's own hometown of Hollywood, California. He is shunned by most of the production houses as any movie in which he acts will not be given permission to air in China, a lucrative market for American cinema. In fact, the second biggest box office market after the US itself. To quote him: "I recently had an episode where someone said they could not finance a film with me because it would upset the Chinese"[69].

To conclude this chapter, I will first admit that I have barely done justice to the topics raised. Each and every one of these can have an entire volume dedicated to it: the Great Leap Forward, the Cultural Revolution, the marginalization of minorities, denying of basic freedoms or the persecution of dissenters. The Communist Party's rule has literally been written in blood.

If China can do this today when it is still in second place, imagine what it could do when it is at the top. I ask the US baiters and critics to introspect. That the US is not perfect is a given. However, the alternative is an absolute and a totalitarian regime that can go to any lengths to get at you if you dare cross it. That day may soon be on us, though I hope not, and this Book is about how to forever postpone that time when you, especially the non-Chinese readers amongst you, would tremble at the thought of criticizing China.

To tell you the truth, I'm a bit afraid myself. If this Book sells well, and I become famous (knock on wood), I will definitely be a tad worried about the ways in which the Chinese government can get at me. For starters, I will mostly certainly never visit Hong Kong, Macao and never, of course, go to China. I mean, that's a given. I have also given up on my Chinese Smartphone, considering that there have been many cases reported of data snooping, which includes password keystrokes being sent to the Chinese manufacturers, which the CCP has unrestricted access to. I definitely wouldn't appreciate the CCP hacking into my account and deleting my files. Can the CCP do worse; is there a risk to life and limb? I don't know, and I hope never to find out. For sure, it will not be a pleasant experience being at the receiving end of the Chinese Communist bear hug.

V
K-Nomics or just plain Common Sense Economics

In the last two chapters, I have endeavored to bring out the differences in the value systems that the US and China bring to the world table. I may have glossed over some of the negatives of the US and vice versa for China. However, the core argument remains intact. The US can lay claim to a far better narrative than can China, and it would not be much of an exaggeration to state that a world order led by China will thrust us back to the Dark Ages.

The rise of China should be a cause for worry. This is straightforward if you're an American, but as I've tried to bring home, also if you're a citizen of any other nation, including China, especially so if you're critical of the CCP. We should all sit up and take notice. Whatever your animosity towards the US or the wrongs the US has done, when compared to China, there's just no competition.

This Book is about giving specific advice on how the US can counter China.

However, just rattling off advice and asking the reader to blindly trust in it will not do. Thus, in this and the next chapter, I will develop the logic of why I will be saying what I am saying. I consider this to be equally important, if not more so. Plain 'advice giving' by listing the things that should be done will sound like preaching. Thus, before I come to the 'how', I need to justify the 'why'. The next two chapters are dedicated to this.

As can be gauged, especially with data presented in the second chapter, the primary problem facing the US is of an economic nature. Thus, many of my suggestions to prop up the US will deal with that. It is clear that the primary battle the US will have to win will be on the economic front.

Although I would have preferred to give my entire reasoning in this one chapter, I have split it into two. This chapter will deal with the basic principles of economics; what we've learned through years of trying out different economic systems, collecting data, using statistics and in some cases just keeping our eyes open to see what works. For example, one doesn't have to do any complex data analysis or have a degree in economics to conclude by visiting the former East and West Germany, before the fall of the Berlin Wall, to know which system has worked.

I will also be cautioning against the use of what I call 'fancy' economics, which, as I will argue, is the primary cause of the current financial mess the US is in, whether it is the recent mortgage crisis or its astronomical debt.

The chapter after that will deal with the problems of globalization and whether it has indeed benefited the US. I will be arguing against globalization while at the same time taking the position that if implemented correctly, it is indeed a good economic system. This will entail some nuanced arguments, which is why I decided to split the globalization part and devote a separate chapter to it.

In this chapter, I will revisit the fundamentals of simple, plain and common sense economics and how its proper use can create long-lasting wealth for nations while at the same time caution against the dangers of being carried away by modern or fancy economics.

Most of what will be discussed here is established economic theory. However, I firmly believe that even if this has been covered in standard economics texts, somewhere down the line, we've lost our way and have adopted alternate, so-called modern or, what I call, fancy economics. Thus, if nothing else, this chapter will be a collation of the best economic theories that have been shown to work.

As stated, I will be using economic ideas already propounded elsewhere. What has been espoused in this and the next chapter is a concise collection of economic ideas from the hundreds put forth that work, along with a couple of my own thoughts thrown in. Follow these and they'll give you the best shot at prosperity. Thus, the best ideas of Economics when distilled, and a few appended herein, gives us common sense economics or if I were to take some credit, let's call it K-Nomics, with the letter 'K' being the first letter of my name.

Without further ado and a bit of self-indulgence, let's dive straight in and reconsider basic and well-established economic ideas.

THE CONCEPT OF WEALTH AND HOW TO GO ABOUT CREATING IT?

Why are some nations rich and some poor, more euphemistically called developing? The obvious in your face answer would be that richer nations have created more wealth for themselves than their developing counterparts. However, that doesn't explain much. The obvious next question would be; how does one go about creating wealth?

To answer that question, we should start with an even more basic one. What is wealth?

The standard answer in any economics text would be that it represents the value of goods and services that you as an individual or collectively your organization or your country as a whole possesses. Goods and services have an intrinsic value. Someone somewhere will be in need of them and be willing to assign some value to it. That value can be in currency units or, in the simpler case of barter in earlier times, give you something of equivalent value in return. The more the goods in barter that you receive or the more the standardized currency units you get, for all the goods and services that you can provide, the greater your wealth. This applies from the individual level all the way up to the national and even global level.

As civilizations grew and the barter system became cumbersome and inefficient, standardized units of wealth like coins were introduced. They acted as a go-between for goods to be exchanged. For example, to trade a whole sheep for a loaf of bread would be quite difficult. For where would I find a bread maker who would want a sheep and what am I to do with so many loaves of bread which one sheep would buy? Better to trade the sheep for standardized units and then spend it little by little to buy loaves of bread whenever I need them. Currency units were divisible, universal and non-perishable, thus making it ideal for transactions and marked a giant leap forward from the old barter system. However, at its heart, the argument is that goods and services have an economic value and can be traded because someone somewhere will be in need of them and will be willing to part with some of their wealth to acquire them. That sum total of the goods and services that you possess and can trade is the wealth you have and the more of it you have, the greater your wealth.

Most countries in the pre-industrialized era were roughly uniformly rich or rather uniformly poor. It was the Industrial Revolution that generated the largest quantum of wealth and countries that were early to embrace this are some of the wealthiest nations today.

Coming to the question of how to go about generating wealth: The answer in its simplest form would be to increase the intrinsic value of the goods and services in your possession. It would, in the earlier example, merely mean to have more sheep or more loaves of bread.

Specifically, ask an economist to list the various means by which wealth can be generated, and the listing would be roughly as I enumerate below. At this stage, I am listing the standard items without explaining exactly how they go about representing or creating wealth. I ask the reader's indulgence in accepting this list. The explanation of how wealth is generated by each of the items listed below will be explained later in the chapter.

Agricultural production

The more the crops you have, the more equivalent goods you can exchange them for and the greater is your wealth. In fact, historically, this has been the primary method of wealth creation that led humankind from being hunter gatherers to settling into villages, which eventually gave rise to the civilizations of the ancient world. They were based on agriculture as the prime generator of wealth. However, it has been superseded in the sheer quantum of wealth that can be produced by one other method, being manufacturing as I explain later.

Improving Human Skills

Improving human skills is another way to generate wealth. A qualified engineer or a physician will have services to offer that have a higher intrinsic value than a high school graduate or an illiterate. Even in the old days, a carpenter had some intrinsic value because of his skills. However, as will be argued later, this is not a great way to generate wealth.

It may come as a surprise to the reader, as it is commonly accepted that improving human skills is the sure-fire way of adding economic value. However, the key ingredient required is the avenues in which these human skills can be gainfully employed to generate wealth, and if that is missing, human skills on their own aren't of much use.

Services Sector

Let's come to the services part of the goods and services traded to generate wealth. It will be argued that on an individual level, the service provider, say the doctor who treats patients can, if he/she runs a successful practice, definitely mint money and get rich. However, on a national level, the effect largely cancels out and the wealth generated is minimum as a whole. So much so that, as I'll argue, the much harped on and in vogue service economy that many developed countries are migrating to is largely to blame for their economic ills.

The Pseudo Service Sector

There is no such separate classification in standard economic theory. This bifurcation of the service sector into the regular service sector and the pseudo service sector is of my own making. Generally, these would include services of technology transfers and software development. The reasons for this split will become clearer as the section progresses. It will be argued that they have enormous potential to generate wealth for the entity receiving that technology.

Research and Development (R&D) in Pure and Applied Sciences

Doing R&D is not a direct way to generate wealth but, as will be argued, it is that foundation on which the best method to generate wealth rests.

Stock Markets

The heading should more appropriately be designated as Trading, but as many trades take place on a recognized stock exchange, I've used that word, as it's easier to relate to. Thus, in general, it can mean any market wherein one can trade any number of products like stocks, futures, options, commodities, currency, etc. As will be argued, these markets are an excellent medium for buyer and seller to meet, and can result in price discovery but do not, except in some rare cases, generate wealth. They are mere tools for wealth distribution.

Manufacturing and Industry

I will argue that it is manufacturing that contributes the most to wealth generation and can pull a country out of poverty.

With the list enumerated, let us begin with the explanations. I will start with the last point first, that is, of manufacturing.

MANUFACTURING AND INDUSTRY

Wealth, as stated, is the intrinsic economic value attached to goods and services. Therefore, the bearer of higher value goods is richer. What, therefore, could be the most clear-cut method of generating wealth? It is to employ some process, read manufacturing, wherein goods having lower economic value, read raw materials, are converted into goods of higher economic value, read finished goods. The difference in the value of the finished goods and the raw materials is the wealth generated. This most commonly happens in a factory setting wherein vast quantities of raw material are converted en masse into finished goods. Raw materials have a lower intrinsic value as someone will pay less for them than the finished product. Sand and copper and tar are not worth as much as, say, a wide screen television that gets manufactured using these ingredients.

To reiterate, the difference between the values of these finished goods being manufactured minus the cost of the raw materials consumed, cost of utilities, labor etc. is the wealth that has been created.

Think about this. That mostly mechanical repetitive process, day in and day out that goes on with all of those thousands of products being manufactured, all converting low-value raw materials to higher value finished goods is what creates wealth. Thus, though there are some other ways of generating wealth as will be discussed, it is the industrial capacity of a nation that matters as it contributes, by far, the most to creating wealth.

This may sound simplistic. At a certain level it is, but let not that simplicity blind you to its true potential. History is witness to all those nations who took advantage of the Industrial Revolution to fuel their emergence as global superpowers and provide for high standards of living for their citizens.

As will be argued later, it is this outsourcing of manufacturing and industry by Western nations today, most notably the US, that has led to many of its financial problems and is primarily responsible for the US's economic decline. One of the central maxims for countering China will be for the US to regain its lost manufacturing base.

AGRICULTURAL PRODUCTION

Does agriculture generate wealth? Some will get upset that I am even asking this question. Is there no respect for the farmer who toils under the hot Sun? Furthermore, if the farmers were to all give up, wouldn't we starve? Well, yes, but I want to examine the wealth-generating potential of agriculture from the strict perspective of economics as outlined above. A straight-up answer with regards to starving would be that for the vast majority of our time on planet Earth, we humans as a species lived not as farmers but as hunter-gatherers. Framing was invented relatively recently about 10,000 years ago, which is recent in comparison to the existence of modern humans viz. the Homo sapiens, who have roamed the Earth for the last 200,000 years.[70] That said, I, in fact, do state that agriculture does indeed generate wealth.

It is because farming converts raw materials, which are the seeds, fertilizers, water, land and sunlight through a process of tilling, sowing, watering and photosynthesis to transform the seed into a grain, fruit or vegetable that has more intrinsic value than the seeds and associated raw materials that went along with it. The difference between the seed and the fruit minus miscellaneous costs is the wealth generated. In fact, many don't see it that way, but agriculture is probably the oldest large-scale manufacturing process in the world. It was the prime progenitor of wealth in ancient times that led to humankind abandoning the jungle life to settle into villages that later flourished into the civilizations of yesteryear, be it the Egyptians, the Babylonians, the Greeks or the Phoenicians.

The farmer uses raw materials like seed, fertilizer, water, insecticide and whatever else it takes and applies a particular procedure called farming to get to the finished product, which is the final fruit or vegetable. It may not seem like high technology today, but the process of spreading the seed, tilling the land, watering it, removing of weeds, harvesting and so on—in short, the entire process starting from the seed to the fruit—is an example of man applying a technology called agriculture. It is an industrial process, though not referred to in that way, which takes raw materials and turns them into finished goods using a industry called farming and a technology called agriculture.

The invention of agriculture was one of the greatest leaps forward in humankind's progress through the ages. From hunter gatherers, we settled down to farm. From wanderers, we settled to grow crops, which then developed into villages, the villages into small towns and so on to the pinnacle of modern civilization today.

Thus, the essential point to note here is this. Yes, the technology is primitive, and hence the wealth so generated is comparatively minor as opposed to high-end manufacturing, but the concept remains the same. In this way, agriculture is no different from manufacturing in generating wealth and is a vital organ of the country's wealth generating apparatus.

IMPROVING HUMAN SKILLS

As former President Obama kept on harping, India has far more doctors and engineers than does the US.[71] Is this something to be concerned about? Do doctors and engineers contribute to wealth creation?

Although Obama collapsed these two professions together, and most of us do, I will argue that they are qualitatively different. Of course, they are different in a sense; one treats sick patients, the other designs bridges, airplanes, factories and such. However, I meant it in a sense specifically with regards their wealth generating potential. I will thus de-hyphenate the two as they contribute differently. Medical professionals, specifically, physicians, have been classified as service providers, and I will argue that their wealth generating potential is minimum as will be elaborated later in the discussion on the Services sector.

I focus on engineers here. Engineering talent, if gainfully employed in designing manufacturing plants, setting up industries, factories and allied infrastructure like roads, airports, railways, etc., will generate wealth for the economy because they directly aid in manufacturing which, as was discussed, has the maximum wealth generating potential of all. Thus, they are important as without them the wealth generating apparatus, read factories, and allied infrastructure cannot be setup.

In a similar vein, scientists who do pure science and pure mathematics are also indispensable. They do the science from which engineers build new technologies and products which, when manufactured on a large scale, generate wealth. Thus, but with one important caveat, improving human skills, especially in engineering, sciences and mathematics, is key to creating a wealthy society.

The caveat is such: It goes without saying that these engineers should get an opportunity to do their job. If they are not gainfully employed, if they do not work towards setting up factories and building infrastructure etc., their talents are wasted. I know this is quite obvious, but it has to be said, as I believe we all, including Obama, has missed this point. If all the manufacturing is outsourced to China, then Chinese engineers can be gainfully employed to generate wealth. If there is no manufacturing in the US, just having engineers won't do. As I said, quite a simple argument but at the same time quite simply missed.

Let me state the case of India. We in India had a vast talent pool of engineers. The dream of an Indian parent was to see their child become a doctor or an engineer. Before the economic liberalization and the opening up of the economy starting in 1991 and to an extent even today, there were no real opportunities for these engineers to be gainfully employed. Jobs were hard to come by as the economy was inefficient and State-controlled, and with the absence of private players, there were limited avenues for engaging the vast talent pool of engineers to create wealth. State-run industry was stagnant with minimum capacity addition, with inefficient production and with jobs guaranteed for life for the select few who got in. This was the state of the Indian economy until the economic reforms of 1991. Thus, I repeat, just having engineers won't do if the economic climate discourages industry and competition or in the case of the US, encourages outsourcing to China. It's obvious, but at the same time missed, that these engineers have to be put to use.

I'll give you a personal example. I am a Chemical engineer. Neither I nor the vast majority of graduates from my class are working as Chemical engineers. Most have switched to IT fields, the one bright spot in my country's economy that does any actual hiring of engineering talent.

In essence, yes, qualified scientists and engineers are essential but have to be able to put their talents to good use. Do that and see the magic they work.

SERVICES SECTOR

As has been alluded to earlier, the service sector has been divided by me into two categories; for lack of any other distinguishing word, the plain, ordinary service sector and the pseudo service sector, which largely deals with a onetime service rendered mainly in the form of technology transfers primarily for setting up of factories. This distinction is important, as the contribution of these two sectors is significantly different. Economists have not yet gotten around to making any such bifurcation and confuse the issue by clubbing them together.

The services sector, which as is generally understood, will include services rendered on a continuous basis, many a time in a standardized form by professionals and businesses. These would generally involve professionals like doctors, lawyers, and businesses like travel agents, stockbrokers, retailers etc.

I argue here that the contribution of these sectors to wealth generation is minimal at best. Let's take the example of a doctor. The doctor offers his medical expertise to treat you. Imagine a famous doctor who charges a hefty fee. You'll be treated and you get well, but you have to pay up. That the dcotor will be quite well off, having made a ton of money from their patients, is clear. However, let it be understood that their patients have become poorer by that exact same amount. Every dollar or rupee earned by your doctor has come out of your pocket.

The same logic applies to any service oriented business like a broker or a travel agent. Any amount of money earned by the broker comes at your expense. That a service is rendered is not disputed. I do not claim that the charge is unjustified. However, by using the concept of wealth generation, what is happening here is that wealth is getting distributed rather than actually generated. It's essentially a zero-sum game. For your lawyer to get rich, you, the client, have to get poorer by the exact same amount. The net effect for the country is that one citizen gets richer at the expense of another.

I can imagine the reader complaining that this is a simplistic argument. Yes, to an extent, that would be right. It can be argued that the travel agent who has booked your itinerary has generated some wealth because the random flight schedules can be seen as raw materials and the well-planned itinerary, the finished product, and thus the difference is the wealth generated for you, a part of which the travel agent earns in commissions.

Similarly, it can be argued that although the doctor gets rich at your expense, if he/she were to successfully treat you, the commission earned by your doctor is offset by the intrinsic wealth created. You as a functional human being are a finished product that can then generate wealth for your society, which the same 'you' as the initial raw material, say, sickly and bedridden, can't.

However, let it be understood that the wealth so generated is of an indirect nature and will pale in comparison to the sheer quantum of wealth that can be generated by the endless, repetitive and large-scale hum drum of machines in a factory. The service sector is more a tool for distributing wealth than generating it, with wealth generation, if any, being indirect and minor as compared to manufacturing.

This is bad news for service-based developing economies like India. In fact, a basic comparison of the two economies of India and China will prove the point. India is trying to grow by emulating a service-based model, discouraging industry and shackling it with over-regulation, problems with land acquisition, byzantine labor laws etc. while China is surging ahead with its manufacturing juggernaut on full steam. That China is far ahead of India in pretty much every economic indicator goes to reinforce this point. Further, instead of playing catch-up the difference between these two countries is only widening.

By the same logic, the US too is in trouble. What many economists are calling a 'maturing' of the economy, maturing from manufacturing into a service-based one is, as argued, not good news. Again, China, where the bulk of US manufacturing has been relocated to, is benefiting. The core sector of wealth generation for which the US was once the poster child of, which helped it win two World Wars and which was the pillar of US might has been voluntarily transferred to another country and one whose intentions seem increasingly hostile.

THE PSEUDO SERVICE SECTOR

As alluded to earlier, I've split the service sector into two parts. One is the 'regular' or 'standardized' service sector which delivers predictable services, services rendered on a continuous basis, many a time in a standardized form by professionals and businesses. The other is the Pseudo Service Sector. This sector is traditionally clubbed with the services sector but is different in significant ways. It deals with non-standardized services that are generally rendered one-time instead of on a continuous basis.

It generally includes IT services, technology transfers, turnkey projects, etc. These types of services are highly dependent on project requirements and are provided on a case-by-case basis. Let's take the example of IT services. These should be taken to mean high-end technology and software design rather than call-center outsourcing.

Boeing wanted their planes to land automatically, that is by computer even in poor visibility. They subcontracted the entire technology development program to HCL Technologies, an Indian IT firm.[72] This would by my definition fall into the pseudo-service sector category. It is a non-standard job that is highly project specific. HCL was able to successfully develop this system that gave Boeing the ability to land its planes on autopilot. Of course, HCL would have been compensated by Boeing as per the terms of their contract.

Let's look at it from the wealth generation perspective. For the 'service' rendered, Boeing had to compensate HCL once, and that's the end of it for HCL. The enormous benefit to Boeing is that it can now use this new technology to create wealth, theoretically, in perpetuity. It can mark up the price of its planes, charge a premium, and thus generate wealth for itself on a continuous and ongoing basis like that of a manufacturing plant as it provides a superior product.

In essence, the wealth generated for the company offering the pseudo service is minimal as compared to the wealth-generating potential of the recipient company that can use that pseudo service to generate wealth, theoretically, as stated, forever.

My father runs a technology transfer business in which his company sets up turnkey fertilizer plants. Again, this is not a standardized service as each plant has its own product requirements, throughput, its own equipment setup, etc. Furthermore, this service is rendered one time; that is, the entire factory is set up and then handed over to the recipient to run. This is also a pseudo-service. My dad gets a onetime payment, and that's the end of the deal for him. The recipient company can run the manufacturing plant continuously and generate wealth on an ongoing basis.

Thus, the conclusion is that the pseudo service sector is a non-standardized service that uses high-end human skills and mostly involves a one-time payment for the service provider but which can generate wealth on a continuous basis for the recipient.

The primary reason, I harp on this is such: The US is outsourcing its manufacturing, the primary generator of wealth, to China. This is a sure-fire way of destroying wealth as it leads to wealth generation centers relocating outside of US soil. The US is outsourcing IT consultancy and product development, not just call center jobs, to India. Ignoring call center jobs, which are a continuous service, the main hardcore IT outsourcing is, as argued, resulting is product development and technology transfers back to the US that is, in fact, generating wealth for the US. Let this difference sink in. Indian IT outsourcing creates wealth for the US while Chinese industrial outsourcing destroys it.

Yet, the main bone of contention for many American politicians, whenever they want to decry a loss of American wealth and jobs, is to blame Indian IT companies and let China get away with a clean chit.

RESEARCH AND DEVELOPMENT (R&D) IN PURE AND APPLIED SCIENCES

Pure scientific research is the seed through which the wealth generating apparatus flowers. The reason being that pure research, perhaps not immediately but almost always eventually, gives rise to new technologies which leads to the development of new and better products, which, when mass-produced in factories, generates wealth. In that sense, research is the foundation of future manufacturing which, as argued, is the one sure-fire way of generating wealth.

That man can understand Nature by using logic, rational reasoning and experiment (the scientific method) to prove a conjecture is the greatest leap forward in all of human thought. Most of human existence previously was spent blindly believing in the sayings of your seniors or community elders which morphed over centuries into the many religions of today. By the use of logic and rational understanding, scientists propose a theory which is checked time and again with the observed data. Only when successive experiments support the hypothesis is the theory accepted as true. It is the one guaranteed way of understanding the inner workings of Nature, and I daresay, understanding the mind of God.

Once we understand how Nature works, we can use that theoretical knowledge to invent new technologies that lead to new products having a higher intrinsic value to us. As a rule of thumb, the more high-end the technology, the greater the value difference between the raw materials and finished goods and the greater the wealth so generated. The foundation on which manufacturing rests is technology, and the foundation on which technology rests is pure science and R&D.

However, rarely if ever has pure science found immediate use in technology to benefit humankind and generate wealth. But, make no mistake. If the workings of the universe around us are to be understood, it will not be through mindless beliefs but by asking questions, making conjectures, putting forth theories, using rational thought and argument and then the most essential process of all, testing them in the lab. Once we get to an established theory, the next process almost always starts off, building a prototype of some product based on that theory and mass producing it in a factory to generate wealth.

The factory is that setting, depending on how you take it, that magic box, that celebration of Science that uses Nature's workings to our advantage. Some would say, it is black magic performed by a sorcerer inside a box that converts low-value raw materials to higher value finished goods. Thus, though scientific advancement does not contribute directly to wealth generation, it is the crucible from which new technologies are born and from which large-scale manufacturing can subsequently result. From wanderers and hunter-gatherers to farmers and from that point on to the start of the Industrial Revolution, if we have come this far, it is because of the lead taken by pure science.

Let me give you an example. Let's look at the modern telecom revolution. Pretty much everybody today has a handheld mobile device by which you can talk to anyone anywhere on the globe. Strip that technology back one level, and you have the old landlines of a few decades ago. Go back further, and you get to Alexander Graham Bell, who patented the first telephone. That was the first technology demonstrator, which was mass-produced in factories to get the phones of today.

Go back further and you come to the pure science stage of our modern telecom revolution, that is, in understanding of how electromagnetism works, by the experiments of Michael Faraday and the theory of electromagnetism as propounded by James Clerk Maxwell. It was their seminal contribution to pure science that eventually led to the Smartphone.

It would be remiss of me if I were to not go back even further to the seminal work done not in science, but that absolute pure of subjects, mathematics, and not mention the contribution of Jean-Baptiste Joseph Fourier. His development of the mathematical technique called Fourier analysis (named after him) is the foundation for the analysis of waves of which electromagnetism is a part.

STOCK MARKETS

I could have used the generic term Trading as what I will be discussing here applies pretty much to all trading activities. However, let's stick to the term Stock Markets as it's easily related to and most stock markets nowadays trade a variety of products form stocks to bonds to commodities, Forex as well as derivatives like futures and options on these underlyings.

Strictly speaking, stock markets are not a sector of the economy like manufacturing or services whose wealth generating potential could be discussed. However, it has to a large extent entered into our collective conscious as a symbol of wealth. This is especially so as mature Stock exchanges are considered the epitome of a developed and progressive society. As alluded to earlier, any representation that has anything to do with progress and development, rather than showing the symbols of manufacturing like the wheel and the spanner or a factory symbol with the chimney or even infrastructure like roads and railways as was generally done in the past will now depict the stock markets, the currency symbols and the ubiquitous stocks price graph going up and down in a zigzag fashion but always eventually pointed in the right upward direction. Somehow, the stock markets, the message goes, generate wealth. Trade and you will get rich.

Let's examine this claim in detail in light of the wealth generation argument given above. With apologies for bursting your bubble, I will argue that stock markets are even worse than the services industry in generating wealth for society.

Getting to brass tacks, let's understand that buying and selling is almost always a zero-sum game. Suppose I have Microsoft stock that I sell to you for a hundred dollars and the price goes up to a hundred and five. You made a profit of five dollars per share. Great, but what about me? I have made a (notional) loss of the same amount. The reverse argument applies if the price falls. The net effect of this is zero. Where is the wealth being generated? Similar to the case of the service sector, it is being distributed from me to you.

This argument is not exactly true. The reason being that my loss of five dollars is not an actual loss, as monies haven't been deducted from my account. This is a notional loss or an opportunity loss. This was the profit I would have made if I had kept holding onto Microsoft stock instead of selling it to you. However, the key argument remains. What a market does is distribute wealth from the people who make the wrong trading decision to the people who make the right one.

Furthermore, when it comes to derivatives trading, that is, futures and options on these underlying stocks, this argument is exactly true. Derivatives trading is indeed a zero-sum game. One person's gain is exactly the other's loss. The logic is a bit complicated, but it has to do with the fact that you take hypothetical positions in the traded commodity without actually owning them. Take note that it is this derivates trading that makes up the bulk, more than 90%, of all trades in most exchanges today.

Furthermore, day trading is also a zero-sum game in which the trader buys or sells a particular stock only to reverse and close the position before market close. Again, a zero sum game. Take note again that of all the stock trades, which are anyways in the minority compared to derivative trades, more than 80% of these stock trades are day trades wherein the open positions are squared off by the end of the day.

Again, little wealth, if any, being generated.

Coming to the Microsoft example, when its share price goes up, how much money do you think ends up in that company's coffers? The answer is zero; zip. No benefit to Microsoft. Think about that. Even if the stock price were to go up, the company does not stand to benefit one cent from it.

The company can accrue some benefit if it decides to raise more capital from the markets by issuing a fresh public offering at the higher prevailing stock price. This is known as a Secondary IPO (Initial Public Offering), a nomenclature used to separate it from the Primary IPO or just IPO, which the company issues before the first listing. How often do you think companies come up with this secondary IPO? Rarely, if at all. Most companies have never done it.

Thus, I argue that stock markets are worse at generating wealth than services. In the services sector, the service rendered can benefit the economy and generate wealth, even if indirectly. For example, when a doctor treats you and you get well, you can go about your regular work and contribute positively rather than lying in bed sick.

The stock market cannot even boast of such an indirect wealth generation potential. I am not arguing that they are thus entirely useless. The markets play a different role. It brings together buyers and sellers at one common place, and it is their interplay that results in the most efficient form of price discovery. Thus, it may generate wealth by preventing the destruction of wealth by creating an effective venue for buyers and sellers to meet. The buyer gets the best offer, and the seller gets the best bid.

Thus, all those analysts in their suits and with their six-figure salaries are engaged not in creating wealth but in distributing it. Their efforts, and thankfully not always successful, are directed at making themselves, their company and their wealthy clients wealthier by making the right trading decision at the expense of the average investor at the other end. Again, no wealth creation, only wealth distribution and probably in a way that transfers it from the poor to the rich.

Furthermore, let's understand that the underlying company whose stock or derivative is being traded has to generate a profit for it to command a price in the stock exchange. The core is the business of the company whether it is manufacturing or even services. As I have argued, services can generate wealth, if not overall, at least for the individual or the organization by distributing it favorably into their coffers (the rich doctor, for example). Without this wealth generation, stock prices would be identically zero and the mere act of trading would have no meaning. Let that sink in.

A brief digress, if I may. I would like to talk about the prediction of stock price movements. This has little bearing on the subject at hand but is such a sought-after talent that I couldn't help giving my two bits of experience here. Thus, for those driven to predicting stock prices by looking at charts, analyzing past price volume movements, using indicators like moving averages, my answer is such: it's not possible. To reiterate, to those who swear by Technical analysis as a means of predicting price behavior and profiting from it, the simple answer is that it can't be done.

One of the key realizations of modern economic theory, borne out by actual hard data, is that stock prices, or more accurately, the return series of stock prices, are essentially random. This means that the price movement from one time to the next, from one tick to the next, whether it be up or down and by what magnitude, cannot be pre-determined. An entire branch of mathematics called stochastic analysis has been developed for the study of these random phenomena. That stock prices follow a stochastic (random) process has been well established by studying hundreds of stock price movements over the years. Therefore, just as you cannot predict a coin toss, no matter how many degrees in economics or how many years of trading experience you have, you cannot predict the stock price movement from one tick to the next.

What determines the long-term evolution of a stock price wherein these random effects are averaged out is the underlying performance of the company, that is, its ability to generate wealth. As simple as that.

That brings me to the end of our discussion on the various sectors of the economy and their wealth generating potential.

Let's summarize the key takeaways up to now.

What I have stated here, with a few additions of my own, could be considered standard economic theory, and if I may so state, before modern economics came to the fore. A few more additions and modifications will be made in the subsequent part of this chapter and the next that extend / revisit / collate disparate parts of economic thought to give a consistent and usable whole. Thus, these two chapters can be together dubbed as **K-Nomics.**

To summarize:

The maximum quantum of wealth is generated by manufacturing wherein low-value raw materials are en masse converted into higher value finished goods, the difference in value between the two being the wealth generated. As has been argued, this represents the largest quantum of wealth addition in any economy.

By that same logic, agriculture also generates wealth as it can also be considered a manufacturing process converting low-value raw materials, which are the seeds, to higher value finished goods, the vegetable or fruit grown. However, because of the low-tech nature of this industry, the wealth so generated is limited, and based on agriculture alone, there is only so much an economy can expand and prosper to.

If, as has been argued, manufacturing creates the largest quantum of wealth, investing in pure and applied sciences and mathematics would be the foundation of this endeavor. By understanding Nature's laws and applying them to real-world situations, new products can be invented that have higher economic value, thereby generating wealth. The Industrial Revolution was fueled by the Renaissance in which scientists and other thinkers got increasing free rein to explore and understand the workings of Nature and then exploit her laws by inventing practical appliances to enrich human life. Pure science is essential, and the prime engine through which all wealth is created.

Improving human skills, especially in the core sciences and engineering disciplines, has been argued to be important, as it is from pure and applied sciences and mathematics that the foundation of a manufacturing and industrialized society can be laid. However, just improving human skills without giving an outlet to gainfully employ your engineers to wealth creation avenues would be useless. A classic example would be India before the economic reforms of 1991, and the US, having outsourced its manufacturing abroad, today.

The Service sector as defined here, which includes services rendered on a continuous basis, often in a standardized form by professionals and businesses, does little to generate wealth. The service provided may add value and create wealth, but it is mostly minimal and indirect and, as argued, services are a means of distributing wealth more than generating it.

The pseudo service sector, which is bifurcated from the 'standard' service sector, generally involves services rendered that are highly dependent on project requirements and typically involve a one-time fee. It could include IT services, technology transfers, turnkey projects, etc. As has been argued, it creates minimal wealth for the entity involved in rendering the service but has a potential for generating vast amounts of wealth on an ongoing basis for the recipient entity. This bifurcation was thought necessary, not just for information sake, but to make the reader aware that it is China to which American manufacturing has been outsourced wherein the problem lies rather than Indian IT companies who render a pseudo service which, as argued, generates more wealth for the recipient, that is, the US company than it does for Indian donor.

Stock markets do precious little to generate wealth. Trading is by and large a zero-sum game. It is when the listed company comes up with a secondary issue can they tap the market to raise funds by issuing shares at the higher prevailing stock price and use those extra funds to generate additional wealth. Otherwise, no matter how high the stock price goes, the benefit to the company is nil. Stock markets are important in that they help the buyer and seller meet and provide an effective marketplace for price discovery. It could be argued that they indirectly generate some wealth by helping avoid wealth destruction by minimizing trading inefficiencies.

To summarize, this is the first part of K-Nomics.

The arguments developed here will be necessary, as they will form the cornerstone of the advice given later on how the US can counter China. However, there are a few other aspects of basic economics that are worth discussing which form the other part of K-Nomics, which I'll be taking up here and then with globalization in the next chapter.

LET'S NOT PUT THESE 'EXPERTS' ON A PEDESTAL

Until now, we've discussed the broad sectors of the economy and their wealth generating potential. The principal arguments presented here are based on good ol' common sense. Unlike the experts, I try not to use unnecessary jargon that confuses and obfuscates the issue. As Einstein put it, if your theory is too complicated, it's probably wrong.

Just by looking around us, I would say that the so-called experts have failed us. The economies of the US and Europe, which are increasingly moving towards a service-based model, are slowing down. Not to mention that Japan has been in outright decline for almost a generation now with zero to negative growth. At the other end, China, the industrial giant and poster child of manufacturing is going from strength to strength.

Some economists would argue that China is in its initial stages of growth and, as it matures, it will eventually slow down like the US of today. It has also been argued that there are teething problems in China too. Some have even predicted China's collapse, but that's been talked about for many years already and, at least as of this writing, has not happened. Some say China has an 'over' construction problem, with massive investments in infrastructure that are lying unused. The CCP, in its over-zealousness, has built many cities from scratch. Where there was nothing once but empty farmland, stands a fully developed city, the so-called ghost cities of China. Such is the supply of new apartments that many buildings lie vacant. Not to mention that China suffers from endemic corruption that siphons off a large part of any investment. I can accept that all this could be true, but let's realize this. If China fails tomorrow, it would be because of these mistakes made by the Chinese government of overcapacity and corruption and not because the basic wealth-generation argument as given here is flawed.

My two cents on the future of China is like this. Yes, some infrastructure projects are a waste of resources. However, most will return a good yield and contribute to growth. Even if a few were to be written off, is that such a bad thing? Not really. I'm a citizen of a country known for its creaking and shoddy infrastructure. Having spent my life in India, I've experienced the other extreme of 'under' infrastructure and, trust me when I say this, more is better than less. Any day.

China also has a problem of endemic corruption, but so do many developing countries. However, and this is the key point, the massive wealth generated in China's factories will pull it through because, unlike India or other service-based developing economies, far more is generated than can be realistically siphoned off. China will pull through despite its flaws, its mistakes, and its authoritarian regime because it has mastered that one formula: of creating wealth. At the other extreme, the way things are in the US, which is gravitating towards a service-based economy by having outsourced its manufacturing, even though it may not have rampant corruption as in China, the key progenitor of wealth is missing.

You may be wondering why democracies are losing out to a dictatorship. Simply put, because that dictatorship, read China, has mastered the formula for creating wealth, which is manufacturing. That's the one thing it has gotten right. It's a case study of how a strong manufacturing base can be a backbone for solid and lasting prosperity. It's a wakeup call for the rest of us. We cannot hand over the mantle of leadership to a nation that has offered the world so little other than mass produced goods. We owe it to those who fought for our freedoms, for rule of law, and who overthrew dictators and monarchs. Hence, by the way, the dedication of this Book to the Founding Fathers of the United States. We owe it to them to succeed. Let not this one obvious mistake negate our entire performance and hand the trophy to someone so undeserving. If China becomes the next superpower and enforces its system upon us, it will be one giant leap backwards for humankind. We do not want our children and grandchildren to grow up in a system akin to what exists in China today.

Take note that as long as a country focuses on this wealth creation formula, that country, even if it is in its mature stages of development, will still experience positive growth as new technologies come to the fore that keep contributing to fresh manufacturing and wealth creation. That nation will not end up running huge trade deficits, will not see a flight of capital abroad, will continue to create jobs in-house and will be able to provide a stable and prosperous future for its citizens.

Thus, as a rule of thumb, I encourage a healthy disrespect for these so-called experts. Do not shy away from asking the stupid questions and to keep asking them; especially so if the reply is full of jargon. If the answer cannot be put in a reasonably straightforward manner, there's a good chance it is wrong. It's a good bet that that expert himself has not fully understood the subject and is hiding behind jargon to make their reply sound intelligent.

To the experts who often confidently claim to be able to predict stock price movements, the rejoinder, as previously stated, is that it's not possible. To reiterate, one of the key realizations of modern economic theory, borne out by actual stock price movement hard data, is that stock prices, or more accurately, the return series of stock prices, are essentially random and thus cannot be predicted. Like tossing a coin.

Fundamental analysis, in which one goes through the company's annual reports, balance sheets, profit and loss statements, has a shot at valuing a company and determining a fair price. It is apposite to mention here that the analysis is itself quite involved and one can go as deep as one wants. Even then, a modicum of judgment is eventually required, especially in two things, the first one being the quality of the management cum goodwill of the company. It has to be gauged whether the management will be able to meet the challenges of competition and stay profitable in the future. The second is the extrapolation of today's performance to the future. There are so many unknowns going forward—the market might change, a new competitor may outdo you, the people's wants and desires may change, obsolescence of your product by new technology, etc.—that even when rigorously done, there's no absolute guarantee of success. However, if done well, fundamental analysis gives you, as an investor, the best shot at picking winners.

I would like to talk about the 2008 financial crisis and the role played by these so-called experts.

The 2008 financial meltdown started with the Mortgage crises. Banks essentially started charging lower interest rates when lending to homebuyers. In addition, they also began lending money to riskier buyers, homeowners with poor credit records and whose ability to pay back the loan was suspect. Property prices were going up then. This led the banks to decide that lending to homeowners was not that much of a risk. Basic economics tells us that the lower the risk, the lower the interest charged on that loan and vice versa. In fact, so sure were the banks of the rising property market that they went one step further and offered creative loans to high risk individuals whose ability to pay back, as stated, was questionable. These were known as subprime mortgages, the word subprime indicating that they were lent to riskier or 'sub' prime borrowers. The Chairman of the Federal Reserve, Alan Greenspan, in fact, encouraged banks to offer these adjustable rate mortgages.[73]

In doing so, two rookie mistakes were made by these so-called experts.

The first mistake was the assumption that they were having good times and that they would continue on forever.

The primary risk a bank faces when it lends is default. What if the borrower cannot pay back the loan? The loan becomes delinquent and the NPAs (non-performing assets), the one thing banks hate, increase. That's why lenders, and banks especially, are in general careful when lending out money. Essentially, the reverse happened in the home loan crisis. Banks lent freely to home buyers, so much so that they offered creative loans to subprime borrowers. Why did they do it?

Simply put, because the property prices were going up. The banks figured that even if the borrower defaulted, they could repossess the property and sell it at a higher market rate in the future, thus recovering more than the monies originally lent.

Even an amateur investor will tell you that that's not going to be true always. No market, property or otherwise, will go in any one direction indefinitely. There will be the expected ups and downs. Somehow, the experts, carried away by their own hubris, forgot this fundamental maxim. They forgot that markets go through cycles and kept on lending at increasingly low rates to increasingly risky buyers with that underlying assumption at the back of their minds that if the borrower defaulted, the bank could repossess the property and sell at a higher price in the future, thus recovering their loan.

It's unbelievable, the mistakes made by these financial experts and that too encouraged on by the Federal Reserve. One day the inevitable happened. The market turned. The property market went through a down turn, as all markets do eventually, and when some of the riskier borrowers defaulted and the banks couldn't just repossess and sell at a profit, the NPAs started piling up. This eventually set off a domino effect, exacerbated by leverage (more on that below) that led to the near collapse of the entire banking system, requiring hundreds of billions of dollars of taxpayers' money to bail out.

The second rookie mistake was that of excessive leverage. Essentially, what leverage means is that you can buy something worth more by paying less. Let me give you an example:

Leveraging would occur if you were to buy a stock, technically called taking a long position, worth 100 dollars by paying say $75. That's like 33% ((100-75)/75) leverage. Most brokers allow you to take leveraged positions. In principle, it is not a bad idea. Suppose the price of that stock were to go up to $110. Instead of a 10% profit, your profit stands at 13% ((110-100)/75). However, it's a double-edged sword. If the price falls to $90, the loss percentage is also correspondingly higher. Thus, using leverage, one can take bigger profits while at the same time make bigger losses.

Let's take an extreme case by supposing that the price of that stock were to fall all the way down to $25. You are essentially wiped out as you had put up only $75. If it falls even further, you have to put up fresh monies to keep holding it. However, how often is it that the price of a stock falls from $100 to $25. Not very often. A little leverage is OK as to it would indeed be rare for such a massive price drop.

I repeat, a little leverage is OK as massive price drops are rare.

Suppose you had to put up only $20 to take a position of a $100. Now your leverage would be 400%. If the price went up to $110, your profit would be 50%. That's big. The reverse is also true. If the price went down to $90, you would make a 50% loss, and if it went down to $80, you're essentially wiped out, a 100% loss. If the price were to fall further, you would have to put up fresh capital to keep maintaining your position. You get what's called a margin call from your broker. This is a case of excessive leverage.

Coming to these banks and other financial institutions and their international partners. Not only did they loan monies to risky clients, but they also did it on money they didn't have by using leverage. A bit of leverage, as I have said, is fine, but their leverage ratios were plain crazy. For example, most investment banks had a leverage position of loaning $100 for only 3 actual dollars that they had. That is something like 3000% leverage.[74] In this case, if the investment falls by just 3%, you are wiped out, and that's what happened. The property market corrected slightly and the lending institutions started getting margin calls, which meant that they had to put up more money to maintain their position. Money they didn't have and couldn't raise and the rest, as they say, is history.

Thus, the experts assumed a market, specifically the housing market, which had gone up for a long time in the past would continue to do so, in all probability indefinitely, thus making any loans given even at low interest rates and to subprime buyers essentially risk free as even in the worst case of default, the property could be repossessed and sold later at a higher price, thus guaranteeing a riskless investment. For this supposed riskless investment, they not only put up their entire monies but borrowed heavily at insane levels of leverage, thus ensuring that they stood to be wiped out even if the market were to correct slightly.

That they are these same experts who looked down upon the average Joe and ended up making mistakes even a rookie investor won't, and then had to be bailed out by the same average Joe's taxpayer money in the hundreds of billions of dollars have the audacity to come back wearing those same suits and go about again looking down on that same Joe and proffer him investment advice.

As I say, I encourage a healthy disdain of these experts.

THE GAUSSIAN VERSUS STUDENT'S-T DISTRIBUTION

Markets are inherently riskier than what the Experts predict.

Although inexcusable, as it violates plain common sense, if we were to, with giving every benefit of the doubt to these experts, dig deeper into the reasons for them to have taken such insane risks, it would mainly have to do with the title of this section. Markets are inherently riskier than what the models, which these so-called experts rely upon, predict. It would then be this over-dependence on a 'mildly' flawed financial model without realizing and accounting for its limitations that would take the blame. Let's talk more about it in this section.

Again, I repeat, not that this is any excuse. I firmly believe that there is something of what I call a 'common sense filter' in all of us. If your model is predicting something that doesn't seem right, that's a red flag right there that your model is probably wrong.

At the outset, it would be relatively easy to point out the obvious, and very human, mistakes made. One obvious one is herd mentality. When the markets were rising, everyone was making astronomical profits, courtesy of the excessive leverage positions taken. The temptation was too high to let this opportunity pass, and since the whole gang was partaking of it, there was a fear of being left behind. Furthermore, there was an implicit encouragement, with a much-respected figurehead in Federal Reserve Chairman, Alan Greenspan, who encouraged the offering of these creative loans.

However, a definite reason for why the experts took the risk they took was because their models told them that the risk was, in fact, acceptable, that the risk of default and excessive market movements was much lower than what it actually was in reality. The reason was that most of these financial models assumed that their risk parameters followed a Gaussian, also known as a Normal, distribution, while in reality it follows a slightly different one. Thus, though at some basic gut instinct level, the experts could have realized the insanity of their leverages, it was probably overturned by the modeling figures presented say on some excel sheet or fancy modeling software. Classic case of GIGO (garbage in – garbage out).

For the record, it's been observed that financial variables more closely follow what's known as the Student's-t distribution. Lots of lingo and a funny name, and I'll come to that.

First, lets us start with the Gaussian a.k.a. Normal distribution. Whenever we're dealing with random variables and when one would like to get a sense of how much they will vary, the starting point is to assume that the variations follow a Gaussian distribution.

For example, let's take the case of human heights. Human height can be considered to be random and varies from person to person. If we were to collate human heights from a large sample, it is seen that most heights will cluster around the average or mean. There will be a few who will be tall to very tall and short to very short. To reiterate, most heights center around the average with extremes being rarer the further off we go. If we were to plot this distribution of heights, it would appear bell-shaped. The midsection of the bell having the most area would be where the majority of human heights would cluster around tapering to the ends as we move out. Say the average height is 5 ft 9 in., then most heights would be say within ±3 in. from that, with people shorter than 5 ft and taller than 6 ft 6 in. being rarer. Believe it or not, this distribution first discovered by Carl Friedrich Gauss (hence the name) seems to be a universal law of Nature with many random variables like height, weight, blood pressure, examination scores, rainfall frequency and a variety of other phenomena following this same pattern.[75]

Similarly, economic variables like stock prices (technically the return series of stock prices) all show the

Gaussian distribution to a degree. The phrase to a degree is significant and will be made clear as we progress. Thus, overall a significant milestone was reached when statisticians discovered this distribution, and they could use it to model risk-reward returns and decide as to whether to enter a particular trade or not. It's as if, and I don't want to start a religious debate, God decreed this distribution to model the random workings of our universe. Almost...

It is to be noted that pretty much all financial institutions exclusively use this Gaussian distribution in their modeling. This gives them an indication of where the most likely outcomes will be and how likely or unlikely extreme outcomes are. Based on this information they decide on the trade. Therefore, in a sense, all depends on the accuracy of this distribution. As I have hinted earlier, it works for many things, but for financial variables in general, the Gaussian distribution works only to a degree.

There is another distribution, similar to the Gaussian but subtly different, known as the Student's-t (weird name) which better models financial variables. Before I go into where the differences lie, I would like to digress and share a bit of the historical background.

This distribution was invented by William Sealy Gosset working for the Guinness brewery in Ireland when trying to determine the differences in quality of the beer for small sample sizes. He was prevented from publishing this groundbreaking result by the management at Guinness. He then published it under a pseudonym 'Student'. It could be that the Guinness brewery didn't want competitors to know that they were using a superior distribution for quality control. Anyways, it eventually came out and is considered to be one of the important distributions in statistics, second only to the Gaussian. It should have been called the Gosset distribution but is now referred to by its pseudonym, Student.[76]

It is similar to the Gaussian in that again most values cluster around the mean, and thus it too has a Bell shape. Where it differs is in the prediction of extreme values. It predicts that extreme events will be more likely (for example, very short and very tall people would be more likely) than as predicted by the Gaussian. Of course, this is not true for human heights, and thus the Gaussian models human heights pretty well, but, and herein lies the rub; this is a more accurate description for financial variables. Why is this so, I'm not exactly sure but I'll give my own thinking on this later. To recap, the Student's-t is similar to the Gaussian in that it is symmetric and bell-shaped, but it has heavier tails, meaning that it is more likely to produce extreme values that are further away from the mean.

The key aspect to note, as I have stated earlier, is that both these distributions are similar and almost coincide if placed one on top of the other. They both are symmetric and have a bell-shaped curve, but it is at the tapering end that some of the difference is visible with the Student's-t having slightly fatter tails that don't taper 'fast enough' to the bottom. Mathematically, in addition to the mean and variance that are common to the two distributions, the Student's-t has one added variable known as the 'dof' (degrees of freedom). If the 'dof' is set to infinity, then the two distributions match. For finite values of the 'dof', there is a difference, as stated, towards the tail end.

Whenever the financial modelers, read experts, try to model return series, they invariably use the Gaussian and thus get a far lower estimate of the probability of extreme events happening than otherwise expected from real life, thus, making them feel far more secure than they should. For example, when we talk of the markets gripped by excessive greed and fear, going up or down far more than expected, and for example, they being irrational for longer than we can remain solvent, we are unknowingly referring to the fat-tails of the Student's-t.

Furthermore, and this may surprise many, the financial modelers and the experts in the field know about this. They know that the Gaussian being less fat-tailed does not appropriately model stock price behavior, especially extreme events, and the Student's-t is the more accurate distribution to use.[77][78][79][80][81]

The obvious question then is why do they not use the better Student's-t, when available. The simple answer is that it is much more mathematically involved and complicated to use than the Gaussian. This may sound like a stupid reason and, it rather is. We don't use something that is complicated but more accurate in favor of something less complicated but easy. It's human nature, I guess.

The mathematics of the Student's-t drives away modelers from using it when supposedly these modelers should be good at that one field: mathematics. Talk about taking shortcuts. As the recent crisis has shown, this is one cut too many.

As a specific example, let's take the case of LTCM (Long Term Capital Management) which crashed long before the 2008 financial crisis. It was a hedge fund that traded in options. The experts used the Gaussian distribution to model the risk-returns of options using the Black-Scholes model. In fact, the inventors of this Black-Scholes model were awarded the Nobel prize and were on the board of LTCM. Don't get me wrong. That formula is a brilliant piece of mathematical modeling which allows for pricing of an option. Of the few assumptions in that formula, the biggest one, as you would have guessed, was the assumption of a Gaussian distribution. That the formula represented a major advancement in economic theory when it was first introduced in the 1970s and the brilliance of the two men in getting to it cannot be disputed. However, the unthinkable happened. The Russian bond crises caused an extreme market move that was not predicted by the standard Gaussian (for those who like jargon, it was unlikely to the tune of being a six sigma event as predicted using the Gaussian but actually much lesser by using the Student's-t), and the company had to be bailed. The bailout was in the billions of dollars.[82]

Thus, dear readers, I give you the Student's-t. One of the key takeaways from the financial crisis of 2008 is that the Gaussian is an inadequate distribution to measure risk and under predicts extreme market movements, and a move towards the Student's-t has to be made. From university undergrads all the way to the big banks and other financial institutions deciding on the billions to be allocated, this new distribution has to be incorporated and should supersede the Gaussian in economic theory.

No two ways about it...

Furthermore, an ode to mathematicians, especially statisticians who have given us both these distributions that help us study and understand random phenomena.

I would like to digress a bit here to put forth a theory of mine. It does not relate directly to the subject matter of this Book. However, a few lines; bear with me. What I've noticed is that whenever we study random variables, we generally get a Gaussian distribution for variables that are 'non-living' such as human heights or rainfall density and such. Whenever we study variables that have something to do with human activity such as stock price movements, the likelihood of extreme events is more and we get a fatter-tailed Student's-t. My theory is such. I would like to generalize this concept and state that any activity that stems from some consciousness, whether human or otherwise, would follow a Student's-t rather than a plain Gaussian. Thus, I would like to conjecture that if any random variable displays a fatter-tailed distribution, then there is some underlying consciousness behind it whereupon conscious decisions of a multitude of decision makers is causing the random variable to move around with an increased frequency of extreme events than pure non-living random chance would allow.

Could this, therefore, be used as a test for determining conscious life, and by conscious, I don't mean just high-level human consciousness? Ask a scientist if a cockroach is conscious and they get nervous. How about conducting an experiment involving some activity like foraging for food by a bunch of cockroaches, and somehow measuring some random variable of this foraging, and studying its distribution. If it shows fatter tails, could we then conclude the existence of some consciousness in those cockroaches, no matter how primitive? Extending this further, can this also be used as a test to detect faraway alien life?

As an aside, this also has repercussions on the probability of a nuclear holocaust, an event wherein the superpowers of the world unleash all their nuclear weapons and totally destroy each other and planet Earth along with it. This is known as Mutually Assured Destruction or MAD. Modeling the frequency of this happening by a Gaussian distribution may make it seem to an extremely unlikely event. But we are dealing with human beings who display extremes in behavior far more often, given to bouts of irrational fear or exuberance dictated by the Student's-t. Modeling with the Student's-t, would give the correct and higher probability of such an event happening. For example, the closest we came to **MAD** was during the Cuban missile crisis and that represents one event till date in around 75 years of having nukes. Not so rare, is it? Something the human race should worry about.

I conclude this section thus. The average reader may well claim that I have no idea of these two distributions. The experts, however, 'knew' of these two distributions. They knew that the Gaussian was only an approximation to the real Student's-t. They still went ahead with the Gaussian as it made the mathematics easier, something I would understand if the average Joe would do. Aren't the experts paid to be good at modeling? Anyways, using the Gaussian, they got some absurdly low numbers for the risk that basic common sense, which, I'm sure, all of us possess, would have told them was unrealistic. Regardless, they went ahead with taking insane risks like leverages at a 100:3. Reality intervened when the market moved worse than predicted. They ended up losing their monies and had to be bailed out by the average Joe's taxpayer money.

EXCESSIVE BORROWING AND IS DECLARING BANKRUPTCY AN OPTION?

As has been argued earlier, this trend towards deindustrialization and a move towards a service-based economy is detrimental to the financial health of the US or, for that matter, any country that follows that model. The core message of this Book is that nothing creates wealth like the large scale humdrum of machines acting with the singular purpose of converting low-value raw materials into high-value finished goods. As stated, in the case of the US, this wealth generating apparatus has been largely outsourced to China.

In addition, there is a related issue to contend with, that of spending, or rather, overspending. The US has raked up astronomical debt. In a double whammy of sorts, not only is income not being generated, but also expenses are out of control. In this section, I'll talk about the deleterious effects of the US spending beyond its means.

In principle, spending is not all bad. Without consumers' spending money, there will be little demand for all of the goods and services being offered. I will therefore bifurcate spending into two types. One that can contribute towards wealth generation, the positive spending, and the other that does not so contribute, the negative kind.

Spending money to set up factories, spending monies on infrastructure projects, money spent by the individual to acquire assets and improve skills are all examples of positive spending. Simply put, it contributes to the wealth generation. China excels at this type of spending. Setting up of factories and allied infrastructure has reaped them huge dividends over the past two to three decades with standards of living having improved considerably in that time.

Negative spending is monies spent by the individual all the way to the highest levels of the State that does not have a direct bearing on creating wealth like, say, individuals spending on depreciable assets like fancy cars or a home makeover that they can ill afford and piling on credit card debt, to the State spending on welfare programs that do not directly contribute to wealth creation.

This may sound controversial, but spending on social security and healthcare would fall into this category. Of course, I understand that there is more to a nation than just creating wealth, and some of the responsibilities of a representative government would entail providing for those without jobs and with health issues. Thus, I am not advocating a total ban on such spending. However, what I do say is this. The amounts spent by the US on social security and healthcare are astronomical at 16 and 27 trillion dollars respectively,[8] even when compared with other developed nations at a similar level of affluence. Surely, something is wrong here.

Furthermore, what should happen but is not happening is that such spending, even if done, is not being complemented by spending in other areas that contribute to wealth generation like setting up factories. The US is spending money without any plan of replenishing the monies spent with wealth generated. This results in the classic double whammy of not being able to generate income and spending monies on non-wealth generating avenues. This then forces one to borrow to make up for the shortfall. The net result of all this is indebtedness.

Where does the US borrow this shortfall from? The absolute worst option of a lender; China. The net result of all this borrowing is a total debt in the tens of trillions of dollars, with China holding the majority.[83] China and the rest of the world have been effectively funding this US excess. They have kept on lending over all these years, and the US has just kept on borrowing.

The obvious question to ask is how the US is going to pay back this debt. Former President George W. Bush and Vice President Cheney were unconcerned by this vast accumulation of debt. In fact, Bush presided over one of the largest increases in debt of any president in history.[84] Furthermore, to quote Cheney: "Reagan proved deficits don't matter"[85]. I don't think Reagan ever 'proved' that, and on the contrary, President Reagan was the one continually talking of controlling spending and balancing the books. However, this mindset continues from Clinton to Bush to

Obama and probably even today under Trump. There is no concrete plan by any President to ensure that the US will one day be able to settle its debt. The US keeps borrowing as if there's no tomorrow.

Common sense should tell you this couldn't be right. Can't just go on accumulating debt with no plan or ability to pay it back and expect business as usual. However, do facts on the ground seem to belie this notion? The astute reader may ask the question as to why lenders are continuing to give money to the US. The US is still seen as one of the safest destinations to park your money, and there seems to be no end to the amount investors from around the world are willing to lend. Can't the lenders see that US debt has gone to unmanageable levels and is only increasing? Can't they see that the US government has no concrete plan of payback? I mean, am I wrong and were Bush and Cheney right when they made such a bold claim? It almost seems that lenders are willing to lend as if the enormous debt of the US and its indifference to pay back doesn't matter. Seems like a paradox.

The reason is such: Historically, and even to a large extent today, the US is seen by many as a stable superpower. It is relying on this premise of stability that has existed for the last hundred plus years and especially so since the end of the Second World War, in which it emerged as the dominant nation on earth, replacing the battered economies of Europe, to appeal to lenders to loan it money. The argument is that your money is in the safest and securest possible of locales when it lies in the US Treasury. It is this historical goodwill that the US is banking on today.

However, you can't live on goodwill forever, and increasingly we're hearing voices raised in alarm at this rising US debt.

Let me explain the current scenario by giving a simple example of, say, you lending money to your friend. This will make it easier to understand while at the same time conveying the essence of the argument.

Imagine a friend of yours who has a knack for business. He is running a successful enterprise. In the initial days before starting his work, he asked you for a loan, and you gave him a small amount. At this stage, I am not going into your reasons for you loaning him money. Let's just say you wanted to help a friend. He did well in his business and has since returned your monies with all due interest. It's a win-win for you both. You continue to see him running his business successfully and this inspires confidence in you of your friend's ability.

One day he comes to you asking for more money. Maybe he wants to expand. His proposal sounds like a good bet to you. He makes you an offer and you take it. Based on his past performance and your assessment of him, you lend him more money. Again, he returns your monies with due interest accrued. Again, a win-win.

Imagine that this happens repeatedly over the years, and your friend is as good as his word. You have, by this time, developed a strong bond of mutual respect and trust.

Say for some reason, perhaps different market dynamics, better competition, or just plain laziness on the part of your friend, the most recent time you lent him money, he didn't return it in full or he returned it without full interest. This has happened this once, and you're not much perturbed. We all have our rainy days, and you're ready to overlook this one aberration. This is where the US stands today. Its historical goodwill on paying back debt and its status as the safest destination to park monies, especially since its emergence as a superpower post World War II, have put it in this enviable position. However, it's squandering this goodwill away.

Imagine your friend continuing on this downward slope and failing to return your monies time and again. One day your patience will run out, and you'll just say 'No'. In the extreme case, your friend will have accumulated so much debt with no real ability to pay it back that he will head for the Bankruptcy Court. He will be bankrupt, and you will lose your loaned monies. A lose-lose.

The rules that apply to the average Joe also apply to the big corporations and to nations as a whole.

The US has not yet reached that penultimate stage, but if this callous borrowing continues with no plan for paying back the monies so owed, one day it will. Lenders are relying on the former goodwill of the US as the most prosperous, innovative and stable country, politically, militarily and economically, in the world and in all of human history to keep on this lending binge. But, as should be clear, one can't rely on goodwill alone and hope that things will automatically pan out.

Even if we discount an uninterested US government, what is the long-term plan of the banking institutions, say, the Federal Reserve, to pay back all those loans with interest? One can't just lock it up in some treasury and forget about it.

The generate a return, the US Fed is 'forced' to invest in businesses that could turn out well and repay that loan back with interest. Of course, the Fed does not do that directly. It is the bank of banks. What it does instead is that it loans monies to banks that eventually loan to American businesses all the way from the big corporations to the small Mom and Pop stores. It could be that the monies lent to you by your local bank, if you're in the US, say for buying a car, may have come from your bank borrowing from the Fed which itself has borrowed monies by issuing Treasury bonds. It could well be that those monies can eventually be traced back to China, which is the largest holder of US Treasuries. If you were to now ask, where did China get all that money to buy those Treasuries? It comes from you, the American consumer, buying 'Made in China' goods.

The key problem is that the options for US banks regarding lending are limited. Why? Because the most important source of wealth creation has been subcontracted away and, as argued, the service sector is just not that good at generating wealth. Think about this. It's a serious problem if you're a banker. Where do I invest? In fact, part of the reason banks started this crazy lending binge to homeowners was this dearth of other good investments opportunities in the US. The housing market was the one booming sector, and investing in it seemed like a safe and, even more importantly, the only bet.

Thus, the financial crisis of 2008 was in a sense waiting to happen, and the core issue, therefore, is not excessive lending to high-risk homebuyers at crazy leverages. At a deeper level, it could be that this is a symptom of an underlying disease, that of a dearth of other investment avenues. US banks went through this perfect storm of having few places to park money as manufacturing has been largely outsourced, seeing a booming and historically safe housing market and with encouragement from the Fed, got into this mad scramble of bending over each other to lend monies to subprime homebuyers at low-interest rates. The rest, as they say, is history.

The basic idea is that the US is borrowing monies to fund non-wealth generating avenues rather than infrastructure and industry. Furthermore, some of the new borrowings are going towards interest payments on old loans, always a bad sign. You have to increase income by creating wealth and decrease expenditure to be financially solvent. The rules that apply to the average Joe, to the small Mom and Pop store, to the big corporation to the entire country are essentially the same. Turn a profit or else go belly-up.

Let's entertain even that worst-case scenario. Should the US go belly-up? Should it, like the individual or the corporation, raise its hands and proclaim that it cannot pay back the loans and that the lenders will have to write off the monies lent as bad debt. In short, should the US declare bankruptcy?

Let's examine this option too...

For starters, there is one big difference between the average Joe and Uncle Sam when it comes to declaring bankruptcy. Technically, Uncle Sam cannot go bankrupt. The reason is not that the experts in high places will somehow turn a miracle and salvage the situation. Hardly. In fact, the reader may well be aware of my disdain for these experts by now. The reason is something totally different.

The Federal Reserve is the only institution in the whole country, that is in the US having the legal authority to print money. In the 1970s, we moved away from the Gold standard mandated by the Bretton Woods system wherein monies printed by the government had to be linked to its gold reserves.[86] Probably it was because there was just not enough gold to denominate the entire wealth of nations. Anyways, we moved away from the Gold standard to what is called fiat money. Fiat means by order, or by law. The dollar bill you hold in your hand, or for that matter any currency note of any country today, is money because the US government or the government in that country says it is money and is not backed by gold or any other tangible asset. In short, it is by the order of the US government that the dollar bill in your pocket is money. This gave governments a free hand at printing money. They no longer had to link it to any backed asset like gold.

The 'advantage' of this scheme is that unlike the average Joe, the government could not go bankrupt. The Federal Reserve has the magic beans of a printing press that it can use unhindered. Suppose the Fed bungles up and loses your money. No problem. It just prints more money and retunes your investment along with interest. As simple as that.

Seems magical, doesn't it? Thus, the Fed or the US Government cannot technically go bankrupt. They can borrow as much monies as they want without any worries. If they were to screw up, they can print fresh cash.

This seems to invalidate my above argument of balancing books and using monies wisely to create wealth. It seems that the point I'm making here is that even if I were to use them 'unwisely', I can always come out of the mess. Well, there's a big caveat. If all this seems to be too good to be true, it is.

The critical realization is that printing money does not generate wealth. I mean the Fed, or for that matter, the Central Bank of any government, could, for example, say print a million dollar note and give one to every American, making them all millionaires overnight. Will this work? No. It's a little hard to grasp, but what has to be realized is that wealth has not been generated here. Thus, if everyone were to have a million dollars, the price of a loaf of bread would equivalently go up proportionately to compensate.

For example, supposing there are a 100 dollars in the economy, and you can buy a loaf of bread for 1 dollar. If I were to print an additional 100 dollars, I have doubled the money in circulation. However, this has obviously not led to any wealth creation. The actual buying power of the people remains the same, which would make the loaf of bread cost 2 dollars.

Thus, printing money is no solution. In fact, it leads to runaway inflation. This is the first drawback of excessive printing. The loaf of bread in the above example now costs twice as much, leading to a 100% inflation rate. The second drawback is that your home currency devalues against other currencies as, for example, the loaf would cost more in your home currency than in the foreign currency resulting in devaluation to even out any arbitrage opportunity. As in the above example, if one euro equaled one dollar before this excessive printing, now one euro would equal two dollars.

Thus, unlike the average Joes out there, nations can't technically go bankrupt. However, just printing money is not a solve all. You cause inflation to rise at home. Your credibility is eroded in the eyes of your lenders, and your currency devalues, resulting in the actual payback to the lenders in their home currencies to be less, forcing them to take unwarranted losses. Good luck trying to borrow again in the future. You'll have to pay a far higher interest rate as your country, specifically the US, which was hitherto considered a safe haven is now regarded as a risky investment. The worst-case scenario being of course when investors lose all hope of repayment and plain refuse to lend any more.

Thus, no magic bullet. The effects of bankruptcy and printing your way out of debt have similar consequences. In essence, they erode your credibility and cause financial hardship.

There is no faster way downhill than not creating wealth, spending money as if there is no tomorrow and taking debts not to finance wealth generation projects but to finance expenses and in the worst case, to finance interest payments on previous loans. A perfect storm...

Capitalism versus Socialism: The debate ends here

Capitalism advocates private enterprise, competition, and a free market. Socialism is all for government control over the economy. The State runs the factories, owns the farms, known as collectives, and overall manages the economy.

These two models of economic theory have been and competing against each other for the better part of the past century.

If you ask me, I am an out and out capitalist. I am a firm believer in the capitalist model of free enterprise. Competition gives you lower prices, better services, weeds out inefficient businesses, provides the consumer with choice and overall delivers the best value for money.

It may surprise the reader if I were to say that in the latter part of this Book, I will in fact caution against this free market and free trade ideas championed by the capitalist system, when applied in the context of Sino-US trade. I will be arguing that trade between China and the US is not 'free and fair' with disastrous consequences for the US. In fact, in the next chapter, I will be arguing for a more protectionist stance from the US in its dealings with China, so much so that I will be arguing against globalization. Again, not because I am against the principle per se. On the contrary, I feel globalization has tremendous potential, is a force for good and if implemented correctly can be mutually beneficial to both participating nations. If not, however, it can cause far more harm than good.

Furthermore, recall in the previous sections in which I paint a sorry picture of the current state of the US economy. Couple that with a general slowdown in the world economy with teething problems in Europe with their national bailouts, mounting bad loans everywhere and a British exit from the EU, it would indeed seem that capitalism or the free markets have failed to deliver.

In this section, I will be arguing that this is not so. Capitalism represents the best economic system imagined by the human mind and is far superior to socialism in its ability to generate wealth. However, even this perfect system has some drawbacks. These drawbacks, if not checked, can give rise to the problems we see today. If these outliers of capitalism are properly addressed, then we indeed have invented something of eternal value and wealth generating potential continuing in perpetuity. I will be talking about these outliers in the next section and on globalization in the next chapter.

However, in this section, I will stick to the primary debate, which is that of capitalism and free markets versus socialism and a state-controlled economy. I figure, many would argue that this is one of those debates that would be anachronistic if had today. I agree. These two systems have been tried and tested, and the results are out. However, it would probably surprise the reader to know that there are quite a few people out there, and I state this with confidence that it is indeed so in my own country of India, who still cling on to the old socialist ideals. Thus, for the sake of completeness as part of our discussion will not just be on containing China but how the US can itself generate wealth irrespective of the Chinese threat, I think a brief discussion is apposite here.

The question is; which is the better economic system, Capitalism or Socialism?

Socialism champions state control of assets rather than having private individuals or companies hold onto the means of production. Furthermore, to enforce this system of economic principles, a political organization is generally formed that has near absolute power. A one-party rule was envisaged in which the Communist Party would ensure the implementation and success of this socialist economic system. There was no vote and no party in opposition. Private ownership was banned, and in general, the wealthy industrialists were portrayed as a greedy lot who exploited the labor of the masses. To be fair, at that time in history, there was some merit in this argument. There were no labor laws, and in many cases, workers were made to work until exhaustion with little pay or leave. There was no social security, healthcare or an option to take a day off. Socialism promised workers a paradise wherein everybody would be equal, both politically and economically, and no one would exploit the labor of the working classes. Well, sounds great, at least on paper.

Contrast that to capitalism, which advocated near zero state control wherein an individual was free to work and start a business as they deemed fit, wherein the individual as opposed to the state owned the assets, and it was determined that economic inequality was OK. Those who had a better idea and were willing to take risks and work harder towards their goal had the right to be richer.

Competition was encouraged with the idea that businesses will compete with each other to provide the best service or product with the lowest price to the customer.

It was probably difficult to tell at the beginning, which of these two contrasting economic systems would succeed. In fact, after the Second World War, these two systems had their respective superpower champions with the US on the capitalist and the free market side and the former USSR on the socialist and communist side.

At that time it could have been debated ad nauseam which system was the better one with hard-core proponents on both sides. Furthermore, in the initial years at least, it did seem that the Soviet Union was winning, especially with its high profile space program launching the first satellite, Sputnik, and the first human, Yuri Gagarin, into space.

However, as has been stated before, there is one sure-fire way of determining truth. It's through experiment. Applied in the case of science, it helps in establishing which theory works, and this leads to a better understanding of Nature, which then allows us create new technologies and contribute to wealth creation.

In this case too, something similar actually happened. After World War II, a mammoth experiment of sorts was conducted involving the United States and Russia along with their allies on each side. Millions of citizens from these countries took part in this grand experiment, of course unwittingly so, like guinea pigs, as you pretty much had to follow the system of the country you were born in.

Anyways, consider this grand experiment spanning over many decades from the end of the Second World War in 1945 to the fall of the Berlin Wall in 1989 that involved multiple nations with millions of their respective citizens. A treasure trove of data waiting to be mined, if only information could be made available. One day, with the fall of the Berlin Wall, it was.

With the fall of the Berlin Wall and the free movements of peoples across both sides of the divide, one thing became readily apparent. There was a vast difference between the standards of living of the peoples in these two opposing blocks. Plain as day and night. You needn't be an expert economist or statistician or a finance major to so decipher. The capitalist West was far more prosperous with far higher standards of living than the socialist East. The facts were plain and incontrovertible. One would just have to walk across the border Wall to see the difference.

This was true for all countries, bar none, that followed the socialist model, whether it be countries of Eastern Europe and Russia, North Korea of today when compared to its southern counterpart, or even pre-liberalized India, with its measly 2% growth, famously and depreciatively dubbed the Hindu rate of growth.

Some may argue that it was not socialism that failed. It was that the people of these countries where inherently lazy or dull or had some other flaw. For starters, that's discrimination. Anyways, this is a hollow argument as facts belie this claim. For one, all countries, bar none, that followed the socialist model found themselves in similar penury, and all countries following the capitalist model got rich, even considering the recent market downturns. Thus, to assume that all the lazy folks somehow ended up on one side of this historical divide is hardly credible. Similarly, taking the example of India that had a 2% growth rate before liberalization and around 6%-7% post it, again it cannot be argued that the same people one day gave up on their laziness, rolled up their sleeves and got to work. No. The answer has to be that before liberalization, socialism with its lack of opportunities stifled growth. Only with the opening up of the economy did all those millions of hardworking Indians get that chance to show off their work and better their lives and in doing so raise growth rates and standards of living for themselves and their country.

Let's compare the former East and West Germany. This is one of those clear-cut cases that are seldom found in the otherwise messy historical record. The reason is that these two erstwhile countries were essentially the same Germany before their division post World War II. It was the same country with the same people, same culture, habits, etc. It could not be said that a German ending up on the western side was more hardworking than their eastern counterpart. Alternatively, any argument purporting that East German culture or work ethic or anything else are to blame and not socialism is hardly credible. Comparing these two countries is a statistician's dream. All other variables that could affect the outcome, say, work ethic, culture, etc. are held constant. The only difference, in this example, is that one followed the socialist and the other the capitalist path. Thus, a true apples-to-apples comparison is possible and the conclusions so drawn are free from covariance errors. The inescapable and clear conclusion is that the capitalist system has well and truly trounced its socialist counterpart.

The reason I thought it best to argue this matter is, as hinted earlier, there are many in India and probably across the world who still cling onto this outdated socialist mindset, especially when markets go berserk and capitalism seems not to deliver. They talk about socialism as a viable alternative. Come to think, that one Party that rules China is even named the Communist Party, though it's in name only. In practice, its business model is out and out capitalist with trade with the US the bulwark of its 'get rich' strategy. All of the current prosperity that China enjoys is because of this shift from socialism to capitalism in all aspects except in name.

Thus, although this debate is not directly related to the main topic of this Book, I say to all, that enough is enough. That Socialism doesn't work has been shown time and again and ample data and evidence exists that one would have to be an egotistical fool to continue propounding it.

Acknowledge the sufferings of the millions behind the Iron Curtain, the Chinese peasants under Mao, the Cambodians under Pol Pot and currently the North Koreans under their Dear Leaders. Even if we discount these extremes, Socialism has failed in providing for even the basic necessities due to an inefficient government and bureaucracy which resulted in a reduced standard of living for its people, well below western capitalist standards, with standing in queues for everything being the norm.

One of the primary problems with socialism is the lack of competition. With the State in de facto control of all goods and services, there is no economic equivalent of a political 'Opposition Party' so to speak. This lack of competition stifles growth. There is no incentive to work hard or to innovate. An individual landing a cozy government job at a State-run undertaking could get by with doing the barest minimum of work. There is no competition from your peer working for another company. There is no incentive to work hard or to perform. You get your salary, whether you put in your best or the least required of you. This naturally leads to inefficiencies all over.

Put another way, the biggest problem with socialism is a fundamental error in understanding human nature. Human beings respond to incentive, that is, gain and loss. Remove that incentive, and they have no reason to perform.

Let's take the example of incentive through loss. Working under socialism, there is no fear of my competitors doing better and driving my company out of business with me ending up without a job. With a Worker's paradise and the concept of employment for life, no one can fire me unless I screw up big time. As long as I keep doing the bare minimum required of me without screwing up, I am safe. I will get my salary that will increase year after year as my seniority increases, again, irrespective of the amount of hard work or skill I'm able to bring to the fore. Why should I work anymore than the bare minimum I have to? There is no fear of competition outdoing me, and, let's understand this, fear is a big motivator.

Coming to the other incentive, that of gain. Suppose I am the owner of a company and I do well, have a good business strategy and am willing to work hard because this company is mine and not that of the State, I will put in my best. Take note that there is a big gap between the best a person can do compared to the bare minimum.

Furthermore, if I am an employee, I know that I have to do good or else I could get fired. On the other hand, I may get rewarded by a bonus or a promotion, and if I own stock options, they being directly linked to the performance of my company, I stand to gain if my company does well.

In short, as argued, Capitalism encourages the best in human behavior while Socialism is satisfied with the bare minimum.

There is a saying in the Hindu holy text, the Bhagwad Gita, and I don't want to ruffle any feathers here, but I will say this; the evidence points to it being wrong. The saying goes somewhat like this: 'You should work hard and not worry about the fruits of your work.'

As history has shown, people work with the expectation of the fruit, in most cases the fruit being an increased monetary benefit. If there is no expectation of a reward, people will not work or put in their bare minimum. Incentive drives human endeavor; no two ways about that.

Let's take an example. In India, under the old system, there were only two State-run companies that were allowed to offer telecom services. No private players. What's more, they operated in separate geographic areas predetermined by the government. Thus, even when there were these two companies, they operated in different areas and were not in direct competition with each other. Needless to say, they did a lousy job. The telephone connection quality was poor, and tariffs, especially for long distance calls, was sky high and you had to book your 'trunk' calls hours in advance. There were incredibly long waits before a telephone cable even got installed in your home. On average, the wait times, and I am not kidding here, were around 15 years. The effect of all this was that telecom penetration in India was at abysmal levels.

In 1996, the Telecom industry was deregulated, and private players, both Indian and foreign, were allowed to offer services. As of this writing, with this opening up, India is one of the most competitive telecom markets in the world. Cell phone penetration has crossed the one billion mark. Most carriers today, for a fixed monthly fee of as little as a couple of dollars a month, offer unlimited local and long-distance calling with no roaming charges for both incoming and outgoing calls as well as data packs of 1 GB a day and more. Indians have truly graduated from the 'have-nots' to the 'haves'.

It's therefore time we acknowledge the millions who've led significantly substandard lives under socialism. From almost everyone everywhere in all socialist countries living in a uniform state of poverty, to the extremes of a significant proportion having to eke out a living by scavenging as the Chinese peasants under Mao, the Cambodians under Pol Pot, prisoners in a Soviet gulag and currently the North Koreans under their Dear Leaders, the clear conclusion is that socialism has failed. As I say, the debate ends here.

I end this section with a joke. It's, in fact, a sad joke that reeks of anti-Semitism.

For the record, I do not mean to offend any Jews, and I want to state unequivocally that I have the utmost respect for the Jewish people. What they have suffered under millennia of persecution, the worst being the excesses of the Holocaust, has scant parallel in human history.

This was a popular joke in the former Soviet Union. It chides the State for its inefficiencies and at the same time brings to fore the anti-Jewish sentiment prevailing then, and, I daresay, to some extent even today.

The joke goes like this:

People are standing in front of the local grocery store since early morning. The store is empty. The truck getting the food supplies hasn't yet arrived. This is typical of the State-run inefficiencies of that era. People keep waiting. By twelve noon, the shopkeeper tells all the Jews to leave. "No food for you today", he says. The Jews leave hungry. By mid-afternoon, the truck has not arrived. The shopkeeper orders everyone except Party members to leave. Only Party members now remain. By the way, so much for equality, Comrade. By late evening the truck still hasn't arrived, and the shopkeeper tells everyone, including party members, to leave and shutters his shop for the day. As he is closing his shop, he mutters under his breath, 'The Jews always get the best of everything.'

MINOR DRAWBACKS OF CAPITALISM AND HOW TO CORRECT FOR THEM

In the previous section, I gave my arguments and directed you to the mountain of data available that forces us to draw this inescapable and beyond reasonable doubt conclusion that Capitalism is the far better economic system as compared to Socialism. This grand experiment between Capitalism and Socialism is now done. What is undeniable is that across national boundaries, across peoples and across cultures, wherever this experiment was carried out, capitalism has come out on top.

With this conclusion firmly in place, I take this opportunity to draw your attention to a few drawbacks that exist even in this otherwise almost perfect model of economic theory.

Sometimes, it is these drawbacks that make us question the efficacy of the capitalist system. I have already argued that it is the best system out there, and I doubt the human mind will ever be able to come up with a better one. It brilliantly plays to our strengths as folks who respond to incentives.

However, with the financial crisis of 2008, with many banks and other financial institutions going bankrupt, with people losing a fair share of their investments in equities and in the property market and a general slowdown in the world economy, which has resulted in unemployment and low wages, many question the efficacy of the capitalist system.

As already argued, specifically the 2008 financial crisis stemmed from experts making mistakes a rookie investor would not of assuming the property market would keep rising, borrowing at insane leverages, which their flawed models, though hopefully not their common sense which they ignored, told them was acceptable. Furthermore, at a deeper level, it was having a dearth of other avenues to invest as the most important source of wealth creation had been subcontracted away to China.

This recent financial meltdown has exposed a few chinks in the capitalist armor, a few drawbacks that we have to be vigilant against. If they are adequately addressed, the financial mess of recent years could have been avoided. I have already talked about the use of a more realistic distribution, read Student's-t, to model risk. In this section, I discuss a few drawbacks of capitalism, which are related to discussions already had on the Student's-t. Furthermore, this section should be read in conjunction with the next chapter on globalization wherein it will be argued that though globalization is indeed beneficial, and represents the ultimate realization of the one-world one-market capitalist dream, the way it is being implemented leaves a lot to be desired and in consequence, is doing more harm than good.

Getting to the topic at hand, the first hitch with capitalism is the establishment of a monopoly.

In rare cases, capitalism mirrors socialism. In rare cases, it can happen that there will be just one company that provides goods or services in some particular sector or industry. It doesn't happen that often, but it is possible. That company has become a monopoly. Thus, it's possible, that in such rare cases capitalism mimics socialism in that similar to a State-run monopoly we have a private company as the sole player.

It could be that the company has an excellent product or a great marketing strategy or, and as is not that uncommon, uses its size and market share in a related sector to establish an unfair advantage in the other. Sometimes, it's plain luck. We can expect that in time the monopoly will slip in customer service, inflate prices of its goods, and stop innovating as there is no competition to keep it on its toes.

That this should be discouraged is clear as it defeats the basic tenets of capitalism of not establishing a competitive business environment. How should we go about doing this will be discussed at the end of this section as the solution to this problem and the other issue I will be discussing here overlap to a large extent.

First, let me give you an example of a monopoly. Probably the classic case was that of Microsoft in the 1990s. Microsoft had a monopoly in the OS (Operating System) market with its Windows 95 commanding a more than 90% market share.[87] As readers may remember, it introduced a de facto Internet browser, the IE (Internet Explorer) as standard bundled with its OS. This was in direct competition to the browser offered by Netscape, the Netscape Navigator. Microsoft used its monopoly in the OS segment to force vendor OEM's to offer its own IE over that of Netscape.[88]

Netscape went to Court and the Justice Department ruled that Microsoft was indeed a monopoly.[88] There was a real chance that Microsoft could be broken up with its browsing software, its OS and its popular Office suite, the Microsoft Office spun off into different companies. It would obviously not be fair to allow Microsoft to leverage its OS and Office businesses to snuff out competition in other areas such as the internet browser market.

Eventually, Microsoft was not broken up in a decision of the court that remains controversial to this day. However, what the Justice Department probably failed to do, fate eventually did. To continue the story, during that same time, the only competitor to Microsoft in its OS market was Apple. Google with its Android was nowhere in the picture then.

Apple was pretty much down and out at that time, barely able to hold on with its failed line of products and close to declaring bankruptcy. Steve Jobs, who had been fired previously had just been reinstated as CEO, called Bill Gates and asked him for emergency funding for Apple. Imagine Apple asking Microsoft for money so that it could stay afloat and compete with Microsoft. Of course, at that time no one could have ever imagined that Apple would one-day offer serious competition to Microsoft.

Bill Gates, to everyone's surprise, accepted Steve's offer and pumped in 150 million dollars of emergency funding to help Apple stave off bankruptcy. The reasoning, and I could be wrong, had far less to do with any altruistic feelings Bill Gates all of a sudden developed for Jobs. The reason was that Microsoft was being branded as a monopoly and keeping a competitor in the game, no matter how handicapped, still allowed it to claim that it had competition and was thus not a monopoly as accused.

Of course, I dare say, Bill Gates, nor anyone else for that matter, ever imagined that with this emergency funding, Apple, under Steve Jobs, would bounce back with its iPod, iTunes, iPad, iMac, and the iPhone and eventually surpass Microsoft in market share and one day become the world's most valuable company. Competition is indeed a good thing. In the Smartphone market, Microsoft now comes a distant third behind Google and Apple. In fact, the latest is that Microsoft is withdrawing entirely from the Smartphone segment.

I don't want to prophesize, but had the Justice Department not started this investigation, all of this wouldn't have come to pass. Apple would probably have gone bankrupt, and the genius of Steve Jobs would have been one of those potential what ifs of history.

That's serendipity.

Before I get to the next excess of capitalism, I also want to clarify that Duopolies and Cartels are also sort of a monopoly and the above arguments of them representing the excesses of capitalism hold. I will briefly mention OPEC (The Organization of the Petroleum Exporting Countries) here, which is a cartel and manipulates the price of oil by rigging production capacities. A more detailed discussion is found in later chapters regarding why the US needs to become oil independent which, though it doesn't have a direct bearing on the China angle, caters to the part the narrative of how the US can regain its economic status.

The second excess of capitalism is the exact reverse, which is an overly competitive market wherein the participants are going for each other's throats. This may sound counterintuitive. Why interfere if there is robust competition? Isn't that good for the consumer? Yes, competition is good but, as the saying goes, there can be too much of a good thing.

Let me again give you the example of the Indian telecom sector. Before opening up of the market, as stated, the shoddy performance of these State-run providers was such that, for example, there was a wait of a couple of decades to get a landline installed in your home. Not to mention shoddy service, poor call quality, having to pre-book long distance calls in advance and sky-high telecom rates, especially for long distance calls. However, one could now argue that the tables have turned. For a measly couple of dollars a month, most providers are offering around 1 GB data per day, along with unlimited local and long distance calls and no roaming for both incoming and outgoing. These rates are among the lowest in the world. There's talk of how these telecom operators will ever be able to turn a profit. Already a few operators have closed shop while a few others have merged. With many operators regularly declaring losses, I don't think that these telecom companies will be able to sustain such low tariffs indefinitely.

Can this be considered over competition? Is this healthy for the long-term sustainability of the telecom sector? The answer has to be in the negative. What could happen is that many players will go bankrupt and the remaining few players will then become a de facto cartel/duopoly/monopoly. As a consequence, the rates would probably be jacked back up and the quality of service suffer.

The third excess of capitalism and in fact, so related to the first two that it need not have had its own classification, but for the sake of convenience is separately listed, is that of excessive greed and fear.

A human failing as already put forth on the discussion on the difference between the Gaussian and the Student's-t distribution, the reason for the 2008 financial crisis, and why we shouldn't put 'experts' on a pedestal.

As is stated, stock markets, and for that matter every other market having any tradable security like commodity markets, currency markets, etc., sometimes go through extreme highs and extreme lows. Throughout history, there have been many documented cases of the markets exhibiting extreme pessimism and exuberance. Again, as has been discussed earlier, this is but a manifestation of the Student's-t distribution that allows for more extreme market movements with a higher frequency than the standard Gaussian.

On most days the markets move within the central region of the Bell curve, that is they have minor moves, up and down. It is on rare occasions, again not that rare because of the Student's-, that the markets go berserk. All traders, I'm sure, will remember some nightmarish or euphoric times of this extreme movement.

Coming back to the 2008 crisis, many claim this upheaval as proof that capitalism does not work. No. It just means that capitalism works fine, on most days giving a healthy and competitive environment but on some days, and, as discussed, this probably has more to do with human nature than any tenets of capitalism, the system goes haywire. Thus, to reiterate, all this shows is that capitalism works on most days, unlike socialism that, as argued, does not work on any day. Thus, rather than claiming this as a failure of capitalism, all the above three related excesses of capitalism which is excessive greed and fear shown by the markets to industries and sectors which equivalently can sometimes go through excessive competition one the one hand to monopolies on the other represent the drawbacks of capitalism.

I recommend the common solution to these problems as such: Governments have to establish regulatory bodies whose sole purpose is to monitor a particular industry, sector, or market. Their roles, on most days, will be to sit back and watch. The government should not be in the business of doing business but establish itself as a watchdog. On rare occasions when, say, the market is moving towards establishing a monopoly or where there is a clear perception of unhealthy and excessive competition destroying companies, or when the trading markets move through extremes, does the regulator step in and take corrective measures to redress the problem. Essentially move the market or the industry back to the proverbial central area of the Student's-t Bell curve.

For example, in India, there is the TRAI (Telecom Regulatory Authority of India). If it feels that the market is getting excessively competitive such that the long-term solvency and viability of the telecom sector is at stake, such a regulator should be given the necessary legal teeth to fix prices at a bare minimum level. I am not saying that it should set prices in perpetuity. It should do so for some temporary period until the sector calms down. After that, it necessarily withdraws any such minimum price fixes.

If the regulator feels that a particular sector is moving towards a monopoly, such as in the Microsoft case, it should have the legal authority to take steps to deregulate the industry or, in extreme cases, to even break up the monopoly.

Concerning the stock markets, post the crash of 1929, we already have a regulator; the SEC (Securities and Exchange Commission). However, it's tasked more with catching fraud and making sure companies declare their results in a timely and accurate manner. To avoid potential catastrophic market movements, I also recommend that the SEC be allowed to use what are called 'circuit breakers'. I am not sure if they are in use in the US; they are in the two big Indian stock markets, the Bombay and the National Stock Exchanges. If the price of a stock rises or falls by more than 20% from the previous day's close, trading is suspended in that particular stock for the remainder of the day. Similarly so, if an entire Index rises or falls by more than 10%. Suspending trading activity for the day on large price movements helps calm the markets, and it has been observed that when trading reopens on the next business day, the price reverts back to some extent to the previous day's mean and movements are a lot milder then, thereby restoring normalcy.

Furthermore, there is an alternate regulator of the markets, the Federal Reserve in the US and its equivalent counterpart, the RBI (Reserve Bank of India) in India. However, take note that the policies of the Fed have a gradual impact and cannot be used to curb extreme movements. The Fed regulates interest rates, making borrowing costlier or cheaper and thus controlling the money supply. It can tame an overly exuberant market by raising interest rates and kick-start a stagnant and excessively fallen market by lowering rates.

Both these regulators can work in tandem to ensure that the markets, to put it succinctly, remain in the central area of the Student's-t curve.

Thus, I advocate that the government should maintain an overseer or a mildly regulatory role in each industry and trading market and should establish bodies to ensure a smooth and functioning free market.

In conclusion, the capitalist system of free markets and competition brings out the best in individuals, companies, and society in general. However, due to the pitfalls of human nature, we at times are carried away by excessive greed or fear or put another way, excessive competition or non-competition. To solve this, I recommend the establishment of regulatory bodies in various sectors and markets to step in once in a while to curb this excess to ensure that a smooth and efficient market persists thereby nullifying the few negatives of capitalism.

In short, and this is one of the most important conclusions drawn. Socialism is a failure. Capitalism works most of the time.

However, capitalism with excesses curbed by temporary, and not over intrusive legal fiats by regulatory bodies, is the best of all worlds.

The Main Proposition: Is Globalization Beneficial?

Yes, but with a ton of caveats.

I would say that one of the drawbacks of a capitalist market economy is free trade between nations, a.k.a. Globalization. This may sound counterintuitive. I mean, shouldn't the definition of capitalism and free movement of goods and services taken to its extreme mean free and fair moments of goods across the world, with companies competing not just with their local or national counterparts but also at a global level? Isn't the making of the entire planet one big level playing field, wherein goods and services from across the globe compete, the final aim of capitalism?

Technically, going by its definition, the answer should be an obvious yes. The noble goal of globalization is a worldwide common market wherein individuals and corporations compete to give the customer the biggest bang for their buck. One world, one market.

However, I will argue in the next chapter that this dream has soured, especially so in the context of Sino-US trade, the reason being that the one obvious assumption of globalization being the free and fair movement of goods and services is not upheld. If this free movement is somehow impeded, the entire logic of the benefit of globalization falls through, and, as it will be argued, can end up doing more harm than good to the country at the receiving 'unfair' end.

This tacit assumption of free and fair trade assumed to have been adhered to has been waylaid in all the positive euphoria surrounding globalization.

The argument that the benefits of globalization stand nullified if nations cannot partake of genuine free and fair trade will be the cornerstone of my case against China, and I have devoted a separate chapter to the ills of this one-sided globalization. I will be discussing in detail the problems of globalization, especially when it's not done right, something I call 'pseudo-globalization'. In this section, I present the broad conclusion that globalization has in fact caused more harm than good to the US. I know I am going the other way around of presenting the conclusion before the argument. However, as this chapter is devoted to basic common sense Economics-101 or, if you grant me, K-Nomics, I thought it best to collate all the fundamentals herein before I argue in detail about globalization in the next chapter.

In conclusion, if properly implemented, and I will discuss what I mean by 'properly', globalization does indeed have the potential for tremendous benefit for all. If not, however, it can cause more harm than good, especially, as stated, for the country at the 'receiving' end.

Before I go into the grand debate of globalization and how the US can counter China, I will conclude this chapter by summarizing the key points.

Some may consider my stance as deviating from mainstream economics. However, I don't think it's so much a deviation as a collation of economic ideas that have been shown to work but have probably been waylaid by what I call 'modern' economics. As is the case throughout this Book, I strive to give logical arguments with evidence, whenever available, for supporting my case. A large part of what has been discussed is plain common sense economics. If I can claim some credit here, it would be in distilling what part of economics works, adding a few ideas of my own, drawing conclusions, say, about risk distributions that should have been drawn by now, avoiding technical jargon and complex theories and cautioning against blindly believing in results obtained by complicated formulas without understanding the underlying assumptions made.

I feel like a Judge summing up a case. In most judgments, the final order is short, maybe a paragraph or two containing the innocence or guilt of the accused along with the quantum of the sentence, if found guilty. However, just giving an arbitrary order will not suffice. A judge has to explain their entire train of thought that led to the conclusions drawn, with legal reasoning, shifting through evidence, etc. Judgments have been known to run into hundreds of pages so as to convince the reader of the soundness of the final decision. Once that has been accomplished, the final order is quite short and to the point.

Thus, why something has to be done is more important than how it should be done and hence this chapter. At its worst, it's a plain jotting down of ideas already known. At its best, it is coming up with a few new ideas while at the same time connecting old and established ideas in such a manner as to give a true and coherent picture of economics that works, which can then be used as a foundation for creating a wealthy society.

I have already summarized the first half of this chapter though I purport to give a brief outline again. I have argued as to why I believe manufacturing contributes the largest quantum of wealth generated in society and is an absolute must for any society to get rich. Agriculture too contributes to wealth generation though its useful contribution is limited because of the low-tech nature of the industry. Investing in pure science and mathematics will eventually give rise to new technologies, generating new avenues for wealth creation. Pure science is essential, as it is the prime engine from which wealth is created. It is the bulwark on which future technological developments and then large-scale manufacturing rest upon. To operate these labs we need skilled labor. Thus, investing in improving human skills, especially in the sciences and engineering streams, is essential. Service sector, as is argued, has more to do with wealth distribution than generation. So are avenues for trading like the stock markets. They help buyer and seller meet and eliminate market inefficiencies. However, their role in wealth generation itself is minimal. The service sector has also been bifurcated into the pseudo service sector wherein it is argued that the receiving entity of a technology transfer gets to generate far more wealth than the donor entity.

To summarize the latter half of this chapter.

Market movements are random and governed by a bell shaped distribution. However, the most common one, the Gaussian, does not do a good job of modeling extreme movements. Market extremes are far more common than as predicted by the Gaussian. An improvement over the Gaussian, the Student's-t, does a much better job at this. This particular distribution looks similar to the Gaussian especially in the central area of the bell curve but has fatter tails, meaning it predicts extreme events better. These extremes have to be properly accounted for in any mathematical model of risk, especially one in which the top-level management is allocating billions. The drawback of the Student's-t is that it makes the mathematical model more complicated and thus iterative methods need to be used, as explicit solutions to the equation is not possible. Nevertheless, the one big conclusion that can be drawn from the recent financial crisis is that the Student's-t should be encouraged as the model distribution of choice when analyzing market data.

I encourage a healthy disrespect for the experts and if something sounds too good to be true, it probably is. There is a real human tendency to start believing in your own theory irrespective of whether it is based on sound reasoning or evidence or reasonable assumptions. The experts can get carried away by a herd mentality too, and a dose of common sense never hurt.

It is not bad per se to take a loan. You can use it wisely to generate wealth. However, if you're borrowing without investing in any wealth-generating scheme such as for setting up of factories or infrastructure, then even if the expenditure is on noble causes like social security or healthcare, it's a wasteful expense. What is worse is to borrow monies without any concrete plan of paying it back and then eventually end up borrowing to finance old interest payments. That eventually leads to bankruptcy, in the individual case, or what is similar, printing money at the national level to pay back debt. However, this is not a solve all as it erodes your market credibility, makes borrowing much harder in the future, can result in painful devaluations of your home currency and gives rise to runaway inflation.

Capitalism works, period. Yes, it is the best system we have as it brilliantly plays to our strengths as human beings who respond to incentives and tries its best to curb our negative traits wherein we will give in our bare minimum if not motivated to do something. Competition gives you lower prices, better service, weeds out inefficient businesses, provides the consumer with choice and overall delivers the best value for money.

However, there are a few drawbacks of capitalism. They are in essence the extreme market movements caused by excessive greed or fear and the industry or sector analog of this, establishment of a monopoly at one extreme and unhealthy and destructive competition at the other. In all such cases, I recommend that in every industry and sector and every market, a regulatory body be set up. I am against excessive regulation and am against the government going directly into business. Instead, the role of the regulatory agency would be to ensure a level and fair playing field to all companies. Furthermore, to achieve this goal, in rare cases, the body should have the legal teeth to enforce a break up of a monopoly or to have the players pull back from the brink of competitive destruction or in the cases of a trading market to adjust interest rates and to suspend trading temporarily until markets restore their sanity.

One of the other drawbacks of capitalism is globalization. I understand that this may sound counter-intuitive and, to set the record straight, I am not against globalization per se if practiced in the truest meaning of the word, as will be elucidated in the next chapter. However, as will be argued, especially in the case of Sino-US trade, trading between these two countries is not free and fair, thus defeating the very purpose of having globalized free trade. This is going the other way round of presenting the conclusion before the argument. However, I thought it best to collate the fundamentals here so as to serve as a handy reckoner.

This concludes my two bits of wisdom on wealth creation. In the next chapter, I will talk about the pros and cons of globalization.

VI
Globalization: A dream gone sour

Before we dive deep into globalization, let me set the record straight. I am not against globalization per se. If implemented correctly, it represents the ultimate realization of the capitalist system, involving free movement of goods and services, not just across national boundaries but also around the world, turning the whole planet into a much touted Global village.

However, as I will be arguing in this chapter, the tacit but central assumption herein is; free and fair movement of goods and services. If this is not so, and I will demonstrate that it is not so especially in the case of Sino-US trade, the entire argument for the benefits of globalization falls through.

Before we come to the free movement of goods across international boundaries, let's talk about internal trade first, that is, trade within the nation itself, for example, goods transported across state boundaries, or even, say, across county or city limits. Globalization at the national level would imply, and this is something I strongly support, that governments should ensure easy transport of goods within the country itself, that is, across states, counties, districts or any other administrative divisions. The essential argument being that companies from different parts of the same country can freely compete and the nation, internally at least, becomes one unified entity or market.

The benefits of this internal free trade are evident once you accept the superiority of the capitalist way over the socialist one. The reader may be surprised to know that there are still many countries wherein impediments exist to this free movement of goods across. In fact, this held true in my own country of India before July 2017.

India has a Federated Constitutional structure with States given a wide berth to enact its own internal laws. To move goods across state boundaries, you'd have to pay a State Sales tax and a Central that is, Federal, level VAT. Each state had its own tax schedule, and it was a nightmare to claim credit for taxes paid in one state for goods traveling across multiple state boundaries. Many industry veterans have commented that it was easier to ship goods internationally from India than within the country. Not to mention that though abolished quite awhile back, many cities even had their own tax collection checkpoints known as Octroi, thus adding another layer to the bureaucracy.

Thus, it could be argued that India was not even 'globalized' at the national level. It's only recently with the passage of the Goods and Services Tax (GST) in the Indian

Parliament that the government did away with the Central Sales Tax, State Sales Tax, Excise Duty and Service Tax to enact a single unified Tax viz., the GST by which India has taken its first steps towards being 'globalized' at least at the national level. If we could imagine each Indian state to be an independent country, then it could be said that these States of India today are truly globalized with a genuine free and fair movement of goods across their boundaries.

Before I get into the problems associated with Sino-US trade, for the sake of completeness, let's define, albeit belatedly, what globalization means. Wikipedia calls it 'the process of interaction and integration among people, companies, and governments worldwide'[89]. The European Union refers to it as 'the free movement of goods, capital, services, people, technology and information across national boundaries'[89].

Again, I will focus on this critical phrase; 'free and fair movement'. By this, it should be obvious and understood that both countries should have a fair chance of sending their goods across to the other side. If this is not so, then the very definition of globalization stands voided. I repeat this for emphasis: If this absolute requirement of free and fair movement of goods is not practiced, then the foundational principle of globalization crumbles away, and I then state with supreme confidence that the chief claim of globalization, that of mutual prosperity for participating nations, stands voided.

It will be argued here that Sino-US trade is not 'free and fair' in both directions. It is pretty easy for a Chinese company to export its goods to the US. The other way around, as will be argued, is fraught with unclear laws, dishonest courts, a policy by the CCP which discourages imports and instead forces the US company to set up shop in China followed by, a near certain theft of its trade secrets and that company's eventual obsolescence by a Chinese copycat.

If free trade is not being genuinely practiced both ways, then, in fact, it becomes monopolistic trade, wherein a Chinese company is free to sell its wares in the US but not the other way around. As argued, monopolies do far more harm than good and are the bane of capitalism.

Let's take the example of the colonization of India by the British. The British banned factories in India. All manufacturing was to be concentrated in the UK with the colonies serving as a source of cheap raw materials and a ready market for its finished goods. For example, raw materials such as cotton, iron ore, etc. were transported from the Indian hinterland by railways, built specifically by the British for that purpose and then shipped to the UK wherein they would be processed by their factories into finished goods and shipped back to India. As has been argued umpteen times by now, finished goods have a higher economic value than the original raw materials, and the difference was the wealth generated for the UK. India got poorer and the UK richer. Indians were not allowed to set up factories locally within India. The British banned those with few exceptions. It could be argued that India and the UK allowed for globalized trade with the one caveat being that it was raw materials one way and finished goods, the other. Furthermore, there was no Indian representation in the UK parliament to press for India's rights, say by allowing Indian entrepreneurs to setup local factories. A somewhat similar situation also existed in the American colonies with their war cry being of 'No Taxation without Representation'.

The key thrust of the argument presented here on India is to make the reader realize that when globalization is practiced one way, it has stark parallels to colonization, resulting in more harm than good for the country at the receiving end of the finished goods. An eerily similar situation exists today with regards to Sino-US trade. China actively discourages US imports other than raw materials like farm produce while at the same time pushes for its products to have unfettered access to the US market. Just like in the case of British rule in India, the US finds itself on the losing end of this bargain. India, which was in the past one of the wealthiest places in the world which European explorers competed and sought trade routes for, ended up being one of the poorest by the time of the British exit in 1947. British rule was direct, obvious, upfront and in your face. The Chinese way is more indirect and subtle. However, probe a little deeper, and the similarities should become apparent.

With this background, let me plunge head-on into unraveling this fairy tale called globalization with specific emphasis on Sino-US trade.

Taking things further, in addition to the basic tenet of free and fair movement of goods is another tacit but equally critical assumption of globalization; that of a level playing field between companies across national borders to ensure fair competition. If a level playing field is not preserved between competing companies, it could be that despite its best efforts, the company at a disadvantage will lose out. If I have to run only 30 meters as a handicap and Usain Bolt has to run the full 100 meters, who knows? I may just win. This is another critical and again oft-ignored tenet of globalization, and in a certain sense, probably even more serious than the first one. I'm sure the reader would've come across some news clip or article about some US politician berating the Sino-US trade deficit, without, at the same time, speaking about the unfair advantage enjoyed by these Chinese companies.

In this chapter, I would like to concentrate on this disadvantage first, of how the lack of a level playing field distorts the narrative of globalization. Later on, we will focus on the lack of free and fair movement of goods. Let's start with the minor issues with globalization first and then move on to the big ones.

The first, relatively minor, issue that distorts the level playing field between companies is:

COST OF ENVIRONMENTAL COMPLIANCE

This relates to the amount of environmental damage the Chinese are willing to tolerate to ensure cheaper products. This distorts the level playing field because the competing American company has a much stricter environmental compliance burden. The more the environmental compliance, the higher the cost. Of course, a staunch environmentalist may categorize this as a major issue and I would quite agree. The blatant pollution of Chinese companies has long term consequences for the air, water, and soil quality not only of China but also eventually for the entire planet. However, strictly from the perspective of ensuring a level playing field, compared to some of the other problems that I will be discussing later, the unfair advantage enjoyed by Chinese companies in competition with their American counterparts due to lax environmental compliance is relatively minor.

In general, US companies face stricter norms for environmental control than do their counterparts in China. Furthermore, even when we consider some of these lax Chinese laws, most remain largely unenforced. The factories there each have a Party contact with many of the big ones directly owned by the CCP. The Communist Party, as should be clear by now, is answerable to nobody. It's a dictatorship with none of the checks and balances as are in a Western democracy.

Further compounding the problem is that even if the CCP enacts any regulation, its enforcement is left to local governments who are hand in glove with the factory owners. Compound that with a lack of a free press and an active community of people, be it environmentalists and activists to blow the whistle, the culprits get away with openly flouting norms.

The problem is made worse by endemic corruption. One can pretty much bribe one's way out of anything in China.[90] Of course, if a major catastrophe occurs, then the factory owner is brought to book and made an example of. No escape then. In fact, in such cases, the law will be interpreted to the harshest extent possible to assuage public anger. Nevertheless, while your luck holds, you can get away with polluting with impunity.

The NY Times quoted the Director of the State Environmental Protection Administration, Zhou Shengxian, as saying: "Fraud in project approval was prominent with many projects passing their environmental assessment without fulfilling the necessary criteria."[91]

There are two issues here. One is that this obviously gives an unfair competitive advantage to Chinese companies. The other, that this pollution will one day find its way out of China and harm the environment at the global level.

So widespread is the lax control that even the Chinese Vice Minister Zhang Lijun was investigated for fraudulently issuing quality certificates.[92] Pollution control equipment is expensive and adds to the cost of manufacturing. Chinese companies often maintain scant or no pollution control equipment, dumping their sewage or effluent directly into the sewer or letting the pollutant gases escape into the atmosphere from where they will eventually spread across the globe.

Coming back to the level playing field concept. An American company that follows the strict environmental control policies enacted by its government has to install pollution control equipment such as leaching equipment, cyclone separators, scrubbers and such. This will obviously incur costs, both for installation and operation, and will add to total production costs, thus making its goods less competitive.

The obvious conclusion is that unless China matches up to internationally accepted standards of pollution control and even more importantly demonstrably proves that it is enforcing them, which indirectly will be also doing its harangued citizens a big favor, the US is justified in leveling a pollution tax of Chinese imports.

Thus, to level the playing field between a US company and its Chinese counterpart in this particular aspect of pollution control or the lack thereof, I recommend the imposition of a Pollution Control Tax.

I would end here if not for two possible hurdles that I foresee. These are not arguments against the idea per se but on its implementation. Furthermore, similar objections could be raised on some of the other ideas I will put forth later in this chapter. Therefore, it best to pause and discuss these before moving onto the next problem of globalization, especially, as the solution to this can pretty well be applied to all other cases.

The first problem is the quantity of tax to be imposed. Should it be 10%, 20% or more? The answer is such. It would vary from industry to industry, product to product. The US would have to set up a team that will sort through all industry sectors and determine the amount of monies on average that American companies would need to spend in installing and maintaining the necessary pollution control equipment. The next step would then be to determine the percentage of the product cost that can be attributed to it, and impose an equivalent tax on Chinese imports.

It is time-consuming and probably laborious, but not impossible. In fact, this type of research and record keeping is not uncommon. For example, most countries have a huge complicated customs book that lists pretty much all products ever manufactured along with their import duties. One just has to take it to the next level.

The other issue is whether such a tax may fall foul of some trade agreement, such as the WTO. I'll say this. I am not an expert on all the clauses of the WTO, but for the sake of argument, let's assume it does. The simple answer is, so what? America has renegotiated other trade agreements in the past and can renegotiate this one.

The key understanding and argument to the world at large will be that the US is not doing anything wrong by giving its businesses a fair fighting chance. In fact, other countries may follow suit. I firmly believe that when you're right, there will be others who will step up to support you. Even if this measure falls foul of the WTO, the US should petition for it to be amended or go ahead and unilaterally impose the tax.

In fact, if this tax was levied, I would go so far as to say that the Chinese people, that is, the common man on the street, might even thank the US. It could force Chinese companies to finally become environmentally compliant. Nothing can spur you to action quicker than when your biggest customer refuses to buy your product. Google pollution in China, and you'll see image after image of big chimneys belching out smoke, smog covering China's cities, people wearing masks when outdoors, lakes, rivers, and streams frothing with pollutants and solid waste accumulating in giant heaps.

Even the Chinese President will probably thank you because such are the problems with pollution and so entrenched in the nexus between Party and industry that out of sheer frustration even Xi Jinping once warned that he would "punish, with an iron hand, any violators who destroy ecology or environment, with no exceptions"[93].

How about this; the US imposes a Pollution Tax on Chinese imports that may finally force the Chinese authorities to get serious about getting their pollution under control. By installing proper pollution control equipment and complying with necessary safety measures, the playing field in this one case will be more equal, and China would finally get around to cleaning up its air, water, and soil for which the average Chinese, at least, and everyone else on this planet will be grateful.

I say a win-win.

WAGE INEQUITY

The next handicap suffered by US companies, which again obviously distorts the level playing field, is wage inequity. Chinese workers earn much less than their American counterparts. Not only is their basic wage significantly less, but the competing American company also has to provide for Social Security, probably healthcare and offer some sort of a 401(k) plan in addition to allowing for a five-day work week, eight-hour shifts and provision for sick and causal leaves.

Wages, as should be clear, add to product cost. The obvious solution to this one would be to impose something of a wage inequity tax wherein a similar calculation as to the percentage is done as outlined in the previous section. A value as a percentage of the manufactured cost due to the difference in wages can be determined and imposed as tax on Chinese imports. Again, as discussed in the previous section, it could be a flat rate or vary from goods to goods or industry by industry.

Low wages were one of the main incentives that made American companies move their factories to China. To some extent, wages in China are going up as China prospers and with a stagnant economy and frozen wages in the US, this gap is narrowing. However, it is still substantial.

However, I will admit that I'm on weak ground here as it would be morally and ethically questionable to force Chinese companies to hire at Western wage rates when there is still substantial poverty in China, especially in the rural areas. China may have a high total GDP, but it lags substantially behind on a per capita, that is, on a per person basis. Thus, a moral dilemma exists in that are we penalizing a poor country for, being poor? I am willing to concede some ground here and grant that maybe this wage tax is morally questionable, and I leave it to the reader and to the American citizen to so decide. However, to do justice to this topic of enumerating all that is wrong with the globalization bandwagon, I cannot help but put forth this one.

Is this, as the French would say, a situation senza soluzione? However, I state that it's not so much to fret about strictly from a level playing field perspective. The reason being that in most industries labor as a percentage of the cost of production is going down and can be minimized to a large extent using automation. Human labor can be made largely redundant by machines and robots, thus nullifying the advantage that Chinese companies enjoy.

Furthermore, one disturbing fact that I want to bring to the fore is the mistreatment of Chinese workers. There is a plethora of information already on this subject, and I'll be covering it only superficially here. The pitiable condition of the Chinese worker is well documented. Workers are made to work far more than the stipulated eight hours, are not given any paid leaves and have no employee contribution to any Chinese equivalent of a social security net. Furthermore, their work environments are generally dangerous wherein they are made to stand for hours on end without protective gear as well as subjected to prolonged exposure to harmful chemicals and loud noise.[94]

This is inexcusable. I propose that the US government can make an issue here and impose a tax or at least threaten to do so if the Chinese government does not make concerted efforts to improve workspace conditions. Let's call it a Humane Working Tax. I, thus, recommend a tax on these lines rather than a Wage Inequity Tax. This would not only be morally defensible, and if this tax or even the mere threat of it forces an improvement in working conditions, the Chinese worker at least will be grateful, if not the Chinese government. A win-win again.

With these two 'minor' drawbacks, if they could be called minor, and some would probably disagree, I will move on to the even more serious flaws with the principles of globalization.

THE SUBSIDY HANDICAP

This is a big one. As alluded to earlier, true globalization would require a level playing field wherein companies across the globe can compete as equals. Subsidy would then be the bane of this ideal. China provides utilities like water, electricity, etc., to its companies at discounted rates. It further offers its industries incentives like tax holidays, clear title land that has already been pre-acquired from its citizenry and other such enticements to enable manufacturing at the lowest costs possible. Add on to this, cheap labor and lax environmental compliance, and all this translates into a significant advantage that's hard to beat.

Let's not underestimate this. Getting land from the government for almost no cost, getting utilities for free or at substantial discounts and tax breaks. These add substantial savings to the cost of production. No company, American or otherwise, can hope to compete against this.

I am loathe to admit but, as I have detailed more particularly in my previous Book 'Land Acquisition in India: Is the Farmer Wrong?'[95], the issues with land acquisition is one of the reasons India is lagging behind China in manufacturing despite having a talented and a cheap workforce. The other reason is the substantially high cost of utilities like water and electricity that even when made available is unreliable with frequent cuts. In India, many projects have stalled because of incomplete land acquisition. There have been widespread protests from farmers and other landowners who then demand exorbitant rates for giving up land, in many cases, multiple times the going rate. 'Make in India' is the pet project of the current Prime Minister, Narendra Modi. However, unless these two major issues, that of land acquisition and cost of utilities, are adequately addressed, it's with despair that I say that I do not see his dream becoming a reality anytime soon.

An article in Industry Week cites American steel mills having laid off 13,000 employees due to Chinese dumping of cheap steel. The claim is that China can manufacture steel at much cheaper rates, primarily because of their government subsidies. Furthermore, United States Steel Corporation has filed a lawsuit claiming that the Chinese stole their trade secrets. When China was prevented from dumping steel in the US, they routed it through third countries to avoid penalties and anti-dumping duties.[96]

Of course, the straight solution to this problem would be to impose a Subsidy Tax on Chinese imports that would, like the previous cases, nullify the effects of cheaper utilities and free land. Some would argue that one can hardly complain if the Chinese government is going that extra mile to attract investments and giving their factories a head start by providing substantial ready infrastructure. In principle, I would have to disagree as it defeats the level playing concept of globalization. A few references for the reader.

How Chinese Subsidies Changed the World
Harvard Business Review[97]

The Hidden Advantage of Chinese Subsidies
World Financial Review[98]

WTO investigates allegations of illegal China subsidies
ABC News[99]

Chinese Government Subsidies Play Major Part In Electric Car Maker BYD's Rise
Forbes[100]

The Explosive Rise of Subsidies to Chinese Industry
Information Technology and Innovative Foundation[101]

Perverse advantage
The Economist[102]

Chinese Industrial Subsidies Grow 23%
The Wall Street Journal[103]

China deploys State power to dominate Global Steel industry
Industry Today[104]

However, that said, I do find some merit in the contra argument. Rather than berating China, let's learn from their example. I will be substantially so arguing in the next chapter which deals about how the US can counter China, that it is time for the US to re-industrialize and that the US government should start giving subsides and invest massively in its own infrastructure to give an equivalent competitive advantage to its own companies. Like the Chinese, it is high time America put its own industry back on a pedestal.

THE CHINESE TRIAD OF BUREAUCRATIC BARRIERS, TECHNOLOGY THEFT AND DISHONEST COURTS

Another big one. It pretty much destroys any argument for globalization and exposes Chinese policy for what it really is. Global domination by eliminating the competition, by hook or by crook.

The way the Chinese have structured their trade policy makes it pretty much impossible for a US company to keep manufacturing in the USA. To be clear, I am not the first one to point out the problems faced by American companies who want to export to China. These unfair trade practices have been much explored in literature. Many books and articles have been written on this subject.

In essence, the level to which the Chinese are willing to stoop to, specifically in this case, of eliminating the competition, is shocking. There is a plethora of information available and this section will cover what, at best, can only be considered the tip of the iceberg.

To begin, let's first understand that the Chinese have free and unfettered access to the US market.

However, when it's the other way around, of retailing American products to China, it's an entirely different story. For starters, the Chinese insist that American companies shift their production base to China. The dollops offered are lower wages, tax holidays, cheaper utilities and such. The crucial point is this. If the American company wants to export directly into China, it will find the going tough, what with bureaucratic hurdles and such. In essence, it will be made to see the 'sense' in relocating its factory to China.

The result of this is a mass scale erosion of factories from the US to the detriment of its long-term industrial potential. China has benefited enormously through jobs and, more importantly, through the means of generating wealth having shifted within its shores. Thus, the biggest problem with this type of globalization is the one-way shifting of the wealth-generating apparatus from the US to China and the resulting one-way shifting of finished goods to be retailed in the US.

Finally, when the US company eventually decides to set up shop in China, it will find that there is a different set of hurdles. The parent American company would require knowledge of local byzantine laws, multiple clearances and such. The Chinese government has purposely erected such barriers so as to force the investing American company to tie-up with a local Chinese partner which will navigate the bureaucratic hurdles, the ton of paperwork, myriad permissions and clearances and with filling up of countless forms, and not that I can blame the Chinese for this, in Chinese. The local Chinese partner is many a time hand in glove with party officials.

This entire rigmarole is for a purpose. On paper, China has nothing against free trade, but the grassroots reality is so engineered as to make it impossible for American companies to sell directly into China and for those who then decide to set shop in China, to do so by involving local partners. One could counter that it's best to let the local partner handle the paperwork and take a cut in the profits.

However, it gets worse. In many cases, the local company will eventually insist on some sort of a technology transfer. Reference to some obscure legislation requiring inspectors to access some technology, or maybe the technology transfer will enable them to scale up, or just a basic show of faith. If that fails, there will be threats of stopping production, shutting down the factory and so on. You'd be surprised at how many American companies have acquiesced. Once the technology transfer is affected, as you would have guessed by now, it's bye-bye, parent American company. The local Chinese company will break off its agreement and start producing and marketing the product as if it belonged to it alone.

In sworn testimony to the US Congress, Patrick Mulloy, member of the United States-China Economic and Security Review Commission, stated that because of this theft the US is losing its edge over critical industries like computers and electronics as well as life sciences, biotechnology, aerospace and nuclear technology, which is costing it around 123 billion dollars a year.[105]

Furthermore, as reported by Industry Week, this insistence of the Chinese to set up an R&D unit in China allows simple transfer of technology from the R&D unit to the government. There are more than a thousand R&D centers opened in China by foreign companies, giving them a ready bonanza of the latest research and developments in technology.[105] Such is the level of theft that the Chinese using this stolen technology now feel confident of improving on these designs. They have built the world's third fastest super computer.[106]

Completing the triad with bureaucratic barriers and technology theft are China's dishonest Courts. In some instances, the aggrieved American company may decide to go to a Chinese court. However, as you can imagine, the result is a foregone conclusion. Chinese courts are not known for dispensing fair justice. They are subject to the party dikat. Good luck trying to bring the local company or the party official to book.

Trust China to take this one-step further. Can all this rigmarole of having the American company set up a joint venture in China, followed by technology transfer, read theft, be avoided? Is there a shortcut? Yes, there is always the option of blatantly stealing technology through hacking the original company's database in the US itself.

Thus, if the basic show of faith approach does not work, there is always the option of outright theft. China is engaged in large-scale espionage on US companies. From industrial spying and stealing of patented technology to hacking databases containing private information of ordinary US citizens, to stealing military technology, the espionage covers pretty much the entire gamut. The sheer scale of the Chinese effort is mind-boggling, and the theft, as stated, is not restricted to commercial enterprises but to the private data of American citizens and American military secrets.

The scale is industrial, and when that word gets used in reference to China, it has to be huge. I am sure many of us have come across some newspaper report or such that flags Chinese spying activities in the US. Many US officials have identified China as the leading contender in the stealing of US technology.[107] Of course, it is easy to spy on companies having a unit or a joint venture in China. The mere setting up of that production line would entail the transfer of some technology to the local Chinese company, which would then be handed over to the government. However, in addition to this local spying, as stated, due to the internet and lax security at US firms, spying can be done on companies everywhere and not just on those that are on Chinese soil.

As reported by Time, Chinese government stole trade secrets from companies like US Steel, Alcoa, one of the world's largest aluminum manufacturers, Westinghouse Electrical Company, a leading nuclear power plant technology provider, SolarWorld AG, a solar technology company, to quote just a few. George Kurtz, CEO of CrowdStrike, a private security firm that tracks Chinese government hacking says "Pick a Fortune 1000 and they've all had it happen. They've all been targeted in one form or another or had an incident"[108].

Under the Chinese military, PLA (People's Liberation Army), General Staff Department, 3rd Department, Signal Intelligence, there is a division called 61 Research Institute dedicated to this grand espionage game.[109][110] The game is such: Steal US technology, re-engineer it and then mass produce it locally and have the parent US company go belly up. Many times that product developed in China gets resold back to the US at half the price. The Chinese get for free what the American company probably spent years and millions of dollars in R&D developing. Estimates put the value of this theft at trillions of dollars each year. There is a whole network of labs and other research institutes that convert these stolen technologies into usable designs. To quote Casey Fleming, CEO, BLACKOPS Partners Corp.: "It will not take long for every American citizen to be affected by the scale of this economic espionage assault."

Speaking on this large-scale theft, Richard Fisher, senior fellow, International Assessment and Strategy Center said, "In a sense it is very clear-cut, but we don't want to accept what we see right before our eyes."[111]

The shocking extent of Chinese espionage became apparent recently when it was reported that China implanted tiny microchips in the electronic circuit boards that were sold to companies like Amazon, Apple and even US Government contractors. That tiny chip was the size of a pencil head and had escaped detection all this time. The chip had networking capability and could intercept and transfer data and trade secrets to the Chinese Government. US officials have described this operation as "the most significant supply chain attack known to have been carried out against American companies."[112]

An article in Science states that around 87% of the counterfeit goods that were seized by the US came from China. According to former Director of National Intelligence, Admiral Dennis Blair: "The massive theft of American IP... threatens our nation's security as well as vitality"[113].

In 2009, a cyber attack was launched by China on Google and twenty other companies in what became known as Operation Aurora. The objective was to hack into Google databases and steal personal information, especially of Chinese dissidents. This prompted Google to rethink its China policy with a much more hands-off approach to China. Google has even suggested going so far as to shut its entire China operations and closing its China site Google.cn.[114]

Former FBI Director James Comey, speaking to CBS's 60 minutes said, "There are two kinds of big companies in the United States. There are those who've been hacked by the Chinese and those who don't know they've been hacked by the Chinese."[115]

Let's turn to the UK and take the example of the Rolls Royce Phantom. The Geely Ge is a knock off of the Phantom, costing only 3,000 pounds. It is so similar to its original that few can tell the difference, and was displayed not a few stalls away from the original Rolls at the Shanghai Auto expo.[116] Talk of a not so subtle howdy.

LandWind X7 is a copycat of the JLR Range Rover Evoque. When JLR litigated, typical of the unjust Chinese courts, Landwind was not only not punished, but the court had the audacity to cannel JLR patents on the Land Rover, thus making it legal for anyone to copy their design.[117] Justice, Chinese style.

Here's a list of some the other cars that have been copied in China:[118]

- Ruili DoDa V8 from the Toyota Alphard

- Yema B11 from the BMW i3

- Dongfeng Jigni S50 from the Hyundai Verna

- Changan Lingxuan from the Toyota Innova Crysta

- Jiangnan TT from the Maruti 800

- Victory S10 from the Cadillac Escalade

- JAC P241 from the Mercedes GL Class

- Jonway A380 from the Suzuki Jimny

- Huanghai Aurora from the Ssangyong Rexton

- Huanghai CUV from the Hyundai Santa Fe

- LandWind X7 from the Range Rover Evoque

- Geely GE from the Rolls Royce Phantom

- Lifan 330 from the Mini Cooper 5-door

- Brilliance V5 from the BMW X1

- Hawtai B35 from the Porsche Cayenne

- Shuanghuan Bubble from the Smart ForTwo

- Zotye T600 from the VW Touareg

- Cherry QQ from the Daewoo Matiz

- Dong Feng Motors EQ2050 HMV from the AM General Humvee

- Geely Merrie 300 from the Mercedes Benz C-Class

- BYD T6 from the Porsche Cayenne

- Suzhou Eagle Carrie from the Ferrari California T + Porsche Cayman

- Youxia X from the Tesla Model S

- Shanxi Victory Jinchi X1 from the Cadillac Escalade EXT pickup

- Laibao SRV from the Honda CR-V

- Dadi Shuttle from the Toyota Land Cruiser Prado

- BAIC BJ80 from the Mercedes G Class

- BAIC BC301z from the Mercedes B Class

- Mingjun M3 S1 from the Land Rover Freelander 2

- Diablo VT from the Lamborghini Diablo

- CH Auto Lithia from the Audi R8

- BAIC X424 from the Jeep Wrangler

- Kawei F-150 from the Ford F-150

- JAC A6 from the Audi A6

- Zoyte Z100 from the Maruti A Star

- Leopard Q6 from the Mitsubishi Pajero

- BYD S8 from the Mercedes CLK

- Beijing Auto Shenbao D320 from the Mercedes E Class

- Dongfeng EQ2050 M3D from the Hummer H2

- Zhejiang Jonway UFO from the Toyota RAV 4

- Gonow GX6 from the Range Rover Sport

- Huanghai NCV from the Lexus RX

- Hongqi LS5 from the Old Range Rover Vogue

- Shuanghuan SCEO from the BMW X5 and so on...

Again, BMW litigated this matter in Chinese Court and lost. The Court ruled that the two cars looked different while to any casual observer it would be evident that it is a copy. I encourage the reader to Google the two images.

To recap, China is stealing US secrets, leaving the parent American company without a market by making copycat products at a fraction of the price of the original. Furthermore, it is also involved in flagrant Copyright and Trademark violations by allowing Chinese companies to host logos that are deceptively similar to their American counterparts. For example:

Ploystation instead of PlayStation

Not only are the names similar, but I also encourage the reader to Google up the logos and check out the striking visual similarity.[119]

Mike instead of Nike

Dolce & Banana

Sdidsa

Red Labial

Michaelsift Binbows

Sqmy

Pizza Huh

KFG

Nokla

McDnoald's

Borio

King Burger

iPed[120]

There was a case reported in which they counterfeited an entire Apple product store. Copycat stores of Apple were set up complete with similar branding like copying of the Apple logo, and with the look and feel of an Apple store. So perfect was the imitation that even the employees working there thought it was the real thing.[121]

Where Chinese espionage gets into an entirely different ball game is when it steals US military secrets.

As reported by the Epoch Times:[122]

Dongfan Chung, a Chinese American, stole around 250,000 documents from Boeing and Rockwell, for which he was sentenced to 24 years. He stole the blueprints for the Boeing C-17 Globemaster III, which the Xi'an Aircraft Industrial Corporation used to build the Y-20. Again, I encourage the reader to Google the two aircraft images and check the similarities in their designs.

Chengdu Aircraft Corporation developed the Chengdu J-20, a stealth fighter that is a combination of stolen designs from the F-22 and the J-35. Remember these are fifth-generation American fighters, and are the most technologically advanced having radar-evading stealth capability. To say that these fighters are a game changer is an understatement and will give a substantial edge to those countries that possess it.

The Cai Hong-4 (CH-4), or Rainbow-4 drone designed by the CASC (China Aerospace Science and Technology

Corporation), is a copy of the U.S. MQ-1 Predator, that same drone that became famous in Afghanistan.

HJ-12 anti-tank missile able to target tanks over two miles away manufactured by China's State-owned company, NORINCO, is a copy of the FGM-148 Javelin

The Z-10 helicopter is a copy of the stealthy Sikorsky UH-60 "Black Hawk". In fact, part access to the Black Hawk was given to the Chinese by the Pakistanis. Remember that raid on Osama Bin Laden in which one of the Black Hawks crashed. That crash site was visited later by Chinese officials who promptly took the wreckage away for analysis.

The Dongfeng EQ2050 is a copy of the popular Humvee.

A microwave crowd-control weapon constructed by the China Poly Group Corporation is a copy of the Active Denial System developed by Raytheon.

I will now bring your attention to what is the most audacious theft of all; of US nuclear technology.

China stole nuclear test data accumulated by the US through countless nuclear tests in 60 years of testing before the Nuclear Test Ban Treaty came into effect. The sheer audacity of such large-scale theft, knowing full well the massive retaliation from the US if caught, which surprisingly did not happen in a Chamberlain-like attempt to placate the bully, is shocking. To reiterate, the most detailed nuclear test data in the world, accumulated by the US, is now in China's possession.

Wen Ho Lee, a Chinese American who worked at Los Alamos nuclear lab, stole more than half a century worth of test data on how to perfect the yield in a nuclear explosion. All this was made available to the Chinese for free. Lee, in fact, also admitted to having stolen submarine secrets that would successfully expose the stealth characteristics of the entire US submarine fleet.

Using this stolen nuclear data, the Chinese were able to miniaturize their bomb so that multiple warheads could then be fitted into a single missile to target multiple cities using one missile. When this was made public, to my utter astonishment, then President Bill Clinton decided not to make such a big issue of it, lest it jeopardize trade relations with China.

I ask, has America gone mad? I doubt Chamberlain would have been such a softie. To quote Robert Kagan, a senior fellow at the Brookings Institution and a member of the Council on Foreign Relations: "The administration believes that if we don't treat China as an enemy, it won't become one. Those who recommend a tougher approach, who call for containment of China's ambitions, are usually accused of creating a self-fulfilling prophecy. But what if the prophecy has already been fulfilled?"

Such is the boldness of the Chinese government that when confronted with this nuclear theft, they admitted to having the test data and confirmed that they had miniaturized their warhead based on US designs.[123][124] Bill Clinton not only turned a blind eye to the theft of America's nuclear secrets but is said to have allowed the export of a supercomputer, which enabled the Chinese to test their own nuclear warheads thus effectively wiping off America's lead in nuclear technology.[125] Representative Christopher Cox, Chairman of the House select committee that conducted this investigation, concluded that the Chinese stole the design of the W-88 Thermonuclear warhead, which, to quote him, is "the most sophisticated nuclear weapon the United States has ever built". He further states that this "penetration of our national weapons laboratories spans at least the past several decades and almost certainly continues today"[126]

As reported by Time, China also stole nuclear technology from Westinghouse Electric Company, which included critical designs for pipes and pipe routing, which would enable them to offer world-class nuclear power technology for civilian use without any R&D efforts of their own.[127] They then used this technology to outbid Westinghouse, to bag the contract for setting up of a nuclear power station at Hinkley, UK. Talk of rubbing it in.[128]

Even in the satellite launch business, following a string of failures by the Chinese to launch rockets, the US satellite manufacturers Loral Corporation and Hughes Electronics gave design information that included navigation technology to the Chinese. Most readers probably do not know this, but when India wanted a cryogenic engine for its satellite launch, the same Clinton administration denied this request and also put pressure on Russia to not supply these engines to the Indians. Compare this step treatment of India, a natural ally of the US, to that of China.[129][130]

Even China's supposed close ally, Russia, is not spared in this grand espionage game. As per the US Naval Institute Staff, the:[181]

- Shenyang J-15 Flying Shark Fighter aircraft is a copy of the Russian Sukhoi Su-33

- Hongdu L-15 Falcon supersonic trainer copied from the Yakovlev Yak-130

- Shenyang J-11 is based on the Russian Sukhoi Su-27

- Shaanxi Y-9 Transport Aircraft copied from the Antonov An-12 Cub transport aircraft

- PLZ-05 Self-Propelled Howitzer from the 2S19 Msta-S Self-Propelled Howitzer

- PHL03 multiple rocket launcher from the BM-30 Smerch "Whirlwind" multiple rocket launcher

- WZ-501 amphibious infantry fighting vehicle copied from the Russian BMP-1 amphibious infantry fighting vehicle

and so on...

Let this sink in. This single-minded dedication of the Chinese to copying. As an aside, an ode to Chinese engineers who are able to reverse engineer an entire product, at times as complicated as an entire aircraft, from stolen data. Of course, I'm not saying that's right, but still.

Coming back to the civilian side, China's ultimate goal is to make every American company redundant by stealing their technology, reverse engineering it and setting up a local production facility. This goes well beyond what is traditionally considered spying and has enormous repercussions for the US's industrial and technological superiority.

Xi Jinping, the Chinese Premier, has big dreams for China, but a large part of that dream to make China a superpower, if it is realized, and I hope that it is not, will be built on the backbone of grand theft. China's global supremacy will be built on stolen intellectual capital. To critics of the US, who are silent of this copycat rise of China, I ask this: Would you want such a nation to be at the helm of world affairs, which in addition to all its human rights abuses, as was discussed earlier, in addition to propping up the most repressive regimes on Earth, as will be discussed later, has reached this pinnacle by large-scale theft and deception?

I end this chapter by pointing out the obvious flaws, as discussed, in this utopian idea of globalization, which is oft ignored, or not considered serious enough and even sometimes taken to be a positive thing, supposedly a multi-cultural difference of sorts that should to be celebrated. Couldn't disagree more.

I repeat; when trade between two participating nations is not free and fair for the aforesaid reasons and a level playing field is not afforded to competing companies, the principle assumption of globalization falls through. It becomes more of a one-way trade similar to, say, Britain's trade with India under colonial rule. This amounts to one country getting richer at the expense of the other.

This form of globalization does more harm than good to the 'recipient' country, and I caution the reader from being carried away by the hoopla.

However, if I was asked whether I am totally against globalization, my answer would be such.

If it is practiced in the truest sense of the word, then I am for it. If two trading economies can freely sell their wares to each other, have minimum bureaucratic barriers, do not distort the level playing field by providing excessive subsidies, respect the other's intellectual property rights, do not indulge in mass scale espionage and theft of technology, then I would support globalization and I would say that free trade will genuinely create wealth for both participating nations. Yes, if implemented correctly, and that's a big if, globalization is the ultimate realization of the capitalist system.

A few would argue that what I have listed here as the basic requirements for globalization to work is not realistically achievable in practice. Sounds more like a fairy tale. I would disagree based on two counts as stated below.

First, what China is doing cannot be considered to be the behavior of an honest trading partner. If it were to significantly improve by stopping espionage, respecting intellectual property, reducing bureaucratic barriers and such, I might be willing to let go of wage inequity and maybe even environmental compliance. Therefore, even if the dream of fair trade is not fully realized, some of the drawbacks could be ignored if the other partner is making a conscious effort at wanting to engage in mutually beneficial free and fair trade. However, this is not so.

The second is that I claim that trade between the US and Canada falls into this definition of genuine trading partners respecting the fundamentals of globalization well enough. For example, the US and Canada allow for free and fair movement of goods across their borders, have minimum bureaucratic barriers, do not distort the level playing field by providing excessive subsidies, respect each other's intellectual property rights, have similar wage structures and environmental compliance laws and, most importantly, do not indulge in mass scale espionage and theft. The globalization mantra works well in this case. Their trade is mutually beneficial and has led to shared prosperity for both nations.

We could expand this argument further without diluting the basic requirement much to include countries like the UK, the EU block, Australia, New Zealand, Japan, and South Korea.

Maybe even India. India has protectionist policies, but it is systematically opening up and increasingly allowing for free trade with the West. What works in India's favor is respect for the rule of law, an independent judiciary that will punish intellectual property theft, and a lack of subsidy given to local industry. What again distorts the level playing field is wage inequity and lax environmental compliance. It's a mixed bag. However, the one thing that is most definitely going in its favor and what remains my main argument against trading with China is that unlike China, India does not indulge in this mass scale technological and intellectual theft that is the cornerstone of China's policy to weaken the US and emerge as the new global superpower.

To conclude, in principle, I do believe that globalization is beneficial. However, if it is not practiced in the correct spirit, it is better to not indulge in this 'free and fair' trade and keep tariff barriers sky-high.

Before I conclude, I would cover one possible critique of me having overlooked something. It could be argued that I am being too harsh on China. Aren't many other countries in a similar situation vis-à-vis trading with the US? Many countries, especially so in the developing world, have trade barriers for incoming goods but are allowed to retail freely in the US. Why am I picking on China alone?

The counter-argument again is two-fold. Even if this critique is accepted, let's realize that the quantum of trade that the US has with other developing nations is low enough not to cause heartburn or like in China's case, a heart attack. One of the problems with China is the sheer volume of trade wherein this unfair playing field can no longer be ignored and is detrimental to US interests. The other argument is that no country in the world is engaged in this large-scale unethical copying and stealing of technology, both civilian and military, eventually forcing US companies to go out of business and posing a near-existential threat to US industry.

Let's take the example of Bangladesh, a poor and developing country in South Asia that has export concessions from the US to sell its textiles in the American market. Yes, it could be considered to be a one-way trade as

I don't foresee a smooth and hassle-free path for US companies to retail directly into Bangladesh, what with its corruption, bureaucratic hurdles and such, and to be clear, there aren't that many US companies doing business there. In addition, the level playing field concept is skewed by meager wages and a lack of environmental compliance. This one-way export, I will agree, defeats the purpose of globalization and is, in principle, against US interests.

However, if the Bangladeshi market were opened up to US goods, it could be that Bangladesh would run into huge trade deficits and with its meager foreign exchange reserves not be able to pay for its imports. Its economy would crash.

Thus, in principle yes, the same logic applies to Bangladesh too, but let's cut it some slack. At the very least, Bangladesh wants to represent itself as a genuine trade partner; its trade volume is low enough not to cause serious alarm, is not engaged in whole scale theft of American technology, and does not pose a long-term existential threat to the US like China does.

Coming to the last point, that of irrational fear. The argument goes as such. If the US stops trading with China, will it not harm US interests? Don't they have a substantial trading relationship with China? Aren't their stores flooded with Chinese goods? Can they even survive without trading with China ?

It's regrettable that I do find some merit therein.

However, the counter is such. I will give concrete suggestions on how the US can rise back to its preeminence as an economic and world power and beat China at its own game. With excuses for sounding haughty, I say that if these suggestions are followed, I do believe that the US can come back on top. The next section is entirely devoted to giving concrete suggestions on just this.

The basic core argument that has been developed remains. Trading with China is doing far more harm than good to the US. It is time the US weaned itself off China. If China is providing cheap goods, it is impoverishing America by relocating the wealth generating apparatus outside of it such that the reduced price of the goods is more than offset by an increase in poverty in the US thereby discrediting any argument that trading with China will be cost-effective.

Before I move into the next chapter, let's engage in a thought experiment. Let's imagine that none of the countries in the world engaged in free trade. Globalization falls through, and each country becomes an internal island onto itself. Would that be the end of the world?

Let's consider the USA. Can we not imagine all of the US states to be independent nations? If so, the US is internally a globalized world with each state carrying out free and fair trade with each other, each respecting common laws and protecting the other's intellectual property rights and such. We can also throw in Canada, UK, Australia, and New Zealand if you like. The US trading internally is a perfect example of a globalized world wherein the real benefits of globalization are there for all to see. As I have stated earlier, these fifty states of 'these' United States enjoy basic freedoms that have led to governments of the people, wherein fundamental human rights are respected, and wherein science and technology have pretty much invented most of the things we take for granted today. The US can be thought of as a globalized world having reached the true pinnacle of a politically and economically free a.k.a. capitalist society. Even if no other country participates in this grand experiment, no worries.

Alternatively, imagine if planet Earth was smaller than it is and the only landmass it had equaled the area of the US. Let's assume that planet Earth was the size of Mercury or Pluto. Then this planet has already reached its global potential that globalization in its true spirit aims for. Nothing more is required. It's happenstance that Earth is the size it is. The point here is that like-minded jurisdictions can tie up and the rest are rendered unnecessary and even an encumbrance that are best avoided.

Don't fret if nobody else joins this bandwagon. What you, the people of the USA, have achieved has few parallels in the annals of human history. Be proud of this heritage and don't squander it away on this one mistake of false free trade with China. If China cannot be a responsible member of the global system, no problem. Good riddance...

VII
How the US can beat China at its own Game

We now come to what could be arguably be the most crucial chapter of this Book. The specific steps to be taken to counter China and, in a sense, to resurrect American industrial might. The previous two, that is, the fifth and the sixth, dealt with laying all of the groundwork for the suggestions that I'll be giving herein.

It is crucial that the US win this epic battle, not only for its own citizens but also for all of humanity. The third and the fourth chapters talk about the contributions made by the US and the equivalent lack thereof by China, in incorporating basic freedoms and promoting a recognition of human rights that most of us in free societies take for granted today.

In a judgment of a court, the final or operative order is short and to the point. It deals with the operative part, that is, the sentencing. The main judgment, however, which can sometimes run into hundreds of pages, is the building up of the train of thought to the conclusions. Thus, this chapter will be short and to the point. I will not justify my suggestions any further, as they now follow logically from the principles established and discussed in earlier ones. If the reader disagrees with any ideas put forth here, it should be because they disagree with some earlier premise. The corollary to this is that if the reader has accepted the arguments as developed until now, then they have little choice but to accept the final suggestions as given herein below.

Let me start with each of the points as covered in the last two chapters and summarize them very briefly here, lest you die of boredom:

- Manufacturing: As argued, the largest quantum of wealth is generated through manufacturing. Thus, my obvious suggestion, which by now should be a no-brainer, is that America should reindustrialize. This is the most important message of this Book. An economically healthy nation cannot stand tall without an industrial backbone.

- Research and Development (R&D) in Pure and Applied Sciences: Investing in pure sciences and mathematics will eventually give rise to new technologies, generating new avenues for wealth creation. Pure science is essential and the prime engine from which all wealth is created as it is the mother ship from which future technological developments and then large-scale industrialization are birthed.

- Agriculture: I have argued that agriculture is also manufacturing, though it is a relatively low-tech enterprise. Using raw materials like seeds having a lesser value and applying the technology of farming, we get a finished product; the fruit or the vegetable having higher value. Thus, agriculture is to be encouraged and cherished as it generates wealth, not to mention, of course, that it is what puts food on the table. Thus, though low tech and therefore not having a substantial wealth generating capacity, it is still manufacturing. As a rule of thumb, the more high-end the technology, the higher the value addition and the higher the wealth so generated.

- Service sector: I have split the service sector into standard services like lawyers, doctors, etc. and a pseudo service sector. It has been argued that the general service sector is not an effective method for generating wealth. It has far more to do with transfer and distribution of wealth than actually generating it. America's obsession with it, with the tacit approval from many economists who think that America has 'graduated' from a manufacturing economy to a service economy is, as I have argued, misplaced. It's not graduation but a demotion of sorts.

- Pseudo service sector: This pseudo sector was defined as when some sort of a technology transfer takes place. Although this could be considered as a service rendered, I have bifurcated this type of service from the more standard services as discussed above. A company supplying technology of a particular product, like an IT firm developing software that will help automate some task, falls into this category. The difference between this pseudo service sector and the 'regular' one is that the transferor is generally paid once and the service so rendered is an enabling technology, allowing the receiver to generate wealth on an ongoing basis. It was argued that the transferee obtaining that technology by making that onetime payment could then use it repeatedly to generate wealth by manufacturing that product or automating a task. Thus, the transferee company has the potential to benefit much more than the transferor company. I gave the example of HCL developing software for Boeing to help land planes on autopilot. The US, as I have argued, in fact, benefits from this sort of outsourcing. Thus, instead of focusing on Chinese manufacturing that is impoverishing America, many US legislators, and the American people in general, focus on Indian IT companies stealing their jobs. For the onetime payment made to the parent Indian IT company, the corresponding American company stands to benefit much more. Therefore, I argue that instead of making Indian IT a scapegoat for America's ills, I suggest the US welcome it. What Indian IT has earned from American companies is a small percentage of what the recipient American company can make using that technology time and again. Of course, the usual disclaimer of me being an Indian citizen applies.

- Human Skills: Yes, human skills are relevant in the wealth generating apparatus, especially in the areas of science and technology. Pure sciences, as argued, gives rise to new technologies which when industrialized create wealth. Thus, engineers and scientists who do pure research and then convert it into usable technologies are absolutely essential. Obama was fond of pointing out that India and China have more engineers and thus investing in education is the way out. The strict answer has to be a No. Without a strong industrial and manufacturing base, human talent in the sciences and engineering alone is not sufficient. I gave the example of India, which during most of its independent years had a strong pool of engineers but had mediocre growth rates until liberalization beginning in 1991. Prior to that, government policies did not encourage private industry, and all that talent was essentially laid to waste. Thus, nothing beats investing in industry and manufacturing. However, once that is done, any investment in human skills has the potential to give rise to new technologies and give a fillip to this wealth creation cycle.

- Stock Markets: I have argued that stock market trading is essentially a zero-sum game. In day trading, derivatives and currency trading, which constitutes the bulk of all trades, this argument is exactly true. Thus, stock markets do not significantly contribute to wealth creation. They help in oiling the capitalist system by assisting buyers and sellers to meet, aid in price discovery and such. Thus, though often touted as the symbol of wealth creation, Stock markets have far more to do with efficient wealth distribution and cannot in any way compare to manufacturing as a means of generating wealth.

- Excessive Borrowing: The ability to borrow money depends on the trust the lender has on your ability to pay back those funds with interest. The idea is that monies should be borrowed to generate wealth, enabling the borrower to return the capital with interest and have some left over as his gain. Therefore, to spend monies only on social schemes or, worse, on refinancing old debt is a bad idea. As stated, I'm not against social schemes, but monies spent on funding them should be from the wealth created in the economy, most notably by manufacturing, and not by borrowing. Furthermore, to take more debt to pay off old debt is a classic debt trap. It would be naïve of the US to think that it can declare bankruptcy or print money to come out of its economic woes. It would lead to runaway inflation, currency devaluation and a loss of standing in the world. One cannot just turn one's back to debt and pretend it does not exist.

- A new Risk Model: Markets are more likely to go through extremes than as predicted by the oft-used Gaussian distribution. Luckily, there is a ready, off the shelf distribution already available since the beginning of the twentieth century viz., the Student's-t distribution. The Student's-t is essentially similar to the Gaussian but has fatter tails, meaning it predicts extremes in market behavior to be more likely than the Gaussian and better fits the price return series. The clear and obvious suggestion is that financial analysts who model risk should switch over to the Student's-t distribution. Agreed, it is more mathematically involved, but there's little choice left in the matter. At the very least, responsible institutions like the Fed, the SEC should start insisting on its use and acceptance. Furthermore, if your model predicts risks that feel too low to be true, use common sense and realize that they probably are. Thus, my disdain for experts who knowingly used a faulty model to take insane leverages, betting on a market they tacitly assumed will be forever on an uptick. Furthermore, as stated, price return series follow a random distribution and thus it is nigh impossible to predict the movement of stock prices, based on charts or historical price-volume data. Thus, technical analysis does not work. It is only fundamental analysis, which again is not an exact science that gives an investor the best chance at picking winners.

- Capitalism works and Socialism doesn't with a few caveats: Capitalism works, and there are no two ways about it. That old debate between socialism and capitalism has long since been settled. It's time we accept that socialism doesn't work, if for nothing else than to acknowledge the sufferings, the needs, wants and frustrations of the millions who eked out their life under a defunct and uncompetitive economy, and further to ensure that we do not subject our future generations to this same life of need and want. The suggestion is that the US, which it is doing anyways, should follow this capitalist system. Capitalism, which allows for competition and involves private businesses competing to offer the best service at the lowest price, rewards human endeavor and has been demonstrably proven to be a vastly superior system.

- The few caveats of Capitalism: This otherwise perfect system has a few drawbacks. One is the tendency for extreme market swings driven by excessive greed or fear. As already stated, I suggest establishing regulatory bodies like the Fed, the SEC and others that can curb market excess by, say, implementing circuit breakers, temporarily suspending trading and / or tweaking interest rates to suck money out or pour money into the economy. The other related drawback of capitalism is that, at times, in some sectors there can be monopolies and cartels at one extreme and destructive competition at the other. Thus again, in a similar vein, I recommend establishing regulatory bodies to ensure a healthy competitive market such that the market or industry remains in the central area of the Bell curve away from tail end extremes. I gave examples of monopolies like Microsoft and Cartels like OPEC on the one hand and the example of the Indian telecom market, as destructive competition, at the other. These regulatory bodies should not be in the business of doing business but as overseers, exercising control only rarely and only when the situation so demands, to ensure a healthy and level playing field for all.

- The big flaw in Globalization: Globalization is beneficial if it fulfills some basic criteria; chief amongst them is ensuring a level playing field between two competing companies across international borders. Globalization tacitly assumes a genuinely free movement of goods and services with similar legal institutions in both countries to check fraud / counterfeiting and with both countries respecting each other's intellectual property rights and having a genuine mechanism for redressals of disputes. However, as argued, when it comes to Sino-US trade, this basic idea of a level playing field is so invalidated in so many respects that the benefits of globalization stand voided, and this supposed 'free' trade has become a bane for America.

- Wage Tax and Environmental Compliance Tax: To level the playing field, at the outset, two minor suggestions are given. One is a wage tax to ensure that American companions don't lose their competitive advantage because of something not in their control: higher wages to be paid to American workers. As argued, this may be morally questionable. However, for the sake of completeness, I have to state this obvious bias. I have also argued that instead of a wage tax, a related Humane Working Environment Tax could be levied that could force Chinese companies to provide for a safe and fair working environment to its workers. The second is an environmental compliance tax. American companies incur costs due to the additional environmental compliances as compared to their Chinese counterparts. China is messing up with its own environment and indirectly of the world by not only having lax compliance laws, but by not even enforcing those that exist. Thus, to level the playing field, I advocate the imposition of an environmental compliance tax on Chinese imports.

- Subsidies: This one is also pretty straightforward. To level the playing field, the US should impose a tax to negate the effects of the subsidies and tax holidays given to Chinese companies like subsidized or free utilities, ready land, tax breaks etc. Therefore, it makes sense for the imposition of a subsidy tax. However, as I will be arguing later, it will be better for the US itself to invest in its on infrastructure and give similar subsidies to its companies; what I call 'positive investing'.

- The Chinese Triad of Bureaucratic barriers, Dishonest Courts and Technology theft: This is the main objection to globalization, specifically, with regards trade with China. China forces US companies to establish factories in their country, thereby preventing the American company from directly retailing into China. They then steal that technology, make a copycat product at a reduced price and drive the parent American company out of business. If the US company litigates, it de facto looses. Not to mention the large scale theft of US technology, both civilian and military, directly from businesses and contractors based within the US itself.

The solution to all this is surprisingly simple and all convergent on a single idea. If the US doesn't want this one-way trade in the name of globalization to ruin it economically, the simple answer is such:

GO IN FOR A MASSIVE RE-INDUSTRIALIZATION OF AMERICA.

- Firstly, trumpet to the world and of course, internally, that America is again open to manufacturing. Many around the world have given up on the US as a manufacturing hub and consider setting up a factory in China as fait accompli. The pessimist argument is that there is nothing America can do now. It's too late. Thing is, we all, and especially the average American, needs to be jolted out of this lethargy and pessimism. A bit of propaganda and a firm leadership at the top can steer America back on course. To Americans, I say, you defeated the global superpower of that day; Great Britain. You won two World Wars and the Cold War, sent man to the Moon. I'm sure you can, when the time comes, rally and rise up to the occasion and, what's not that difficult, once again make America an industrial power, something it already was in the past.

- Next, I suggest that American companies that set up in-house manufacturing be given tax breaks to counter equivalent Chinese subsidies. Any loss of tax revenue to the US government will be more than offset when American manufacturing comes of age and the tax breaks expire. Remember, this tax revenue wouldn't have accrued anyways if the American company had gone offshore, say to China. Those companies would then have paid tax in China and not in the US. Furthermore, this in-house manufacturing will reduce the import bill, help reduce the yawning trade deficit and generate employment in house. In a similar vein, as I'll put forth later, the US should provide its companies with subsides, just as the Chinese do.

- Go in for minimal regulatory control. Cut red tape to a minimum and let business get on with what they do. Again, I will say that this has largely already been achieved by the US, it being one of the easiest places of doing business in the world. As an addendum to our discussion on capitalism, I have advocated minimal government control. Government should not be in the business of doing business. It is in the business, as I have argued, of overseeing business to ensure that the wild extremes of capitalism are avoided.

- As stated earlier, impose an environmental compliance tax on Chinese imports. This will make up for the cost of environmental compliance that US companies have to bear and, as argued, could have a salubrious effect in that China may try to clean up its own backyard.

- Go in for subsidized power and other utilities, and invest in infrastructure. As discussed, Chinese companies enjoy an unfair advantage because of the subsidized utilities provided to it by the Chinese government. I have argued for a subsidy tax to be imposed on Chinese goods. That argument holds. However, how about the US, for a change, stealing an idea from China and, like them, giving subsidies to American companies. Give subsidized or free utilities like water, electricity and ready acquired land for setting up factories and industries. This alone will significantly blunt the advantage that China enjoys, giving a fillip to American industry and making American goods more competitive.

- For this America will have to invest heavily in improving infrastructure which at one time was the best in the world but has been crumbling. Massive amounts of spending on new power generation plants, utility companies, infrastructure projects like better roads, harbors, rail networks, and airports will be required. I am not saying America's infrastructure is all bad. For example, the American interstate system is still one of the best in the world. However, wherever lacking, pour money in. Until now, America has been spending monies on non-remunerative projects like on healthcare, social security and to finance its debt. That's bad spending strictly from an economic perspective with due cognizance to the moral issues involved with healthcare and social security. Spending on infrastructure, however, enables American companies to be globally competitive and is good spending. It gives American companies a fighting chance and contributes to positive wealth generation.

To summarize, I firmly believe that by

- Understanding that the largest quantum of wealth is generated by industry

- Encouraging manufacturing in-house

- Moving away from a purely service based economy

- Recognizing that trading mostly distributes rather than generates wealth

- Understanding that extreme events in the market are far more likely than as predicted by our current models, and thus going for better ones, and at the same time inculcating a healthy disrespect for experts, as they too have a very human tendency of getting carried away by the same emotions of excessive greed or fear

- Not borrowing excessively with no real hope of ever paying those monies back, and assuming all will be hunky dory if I were to only declare bankruptcy

- Spending monies on wealth generating avenues like infrastructure and manufacturing

- Realizing the flaws of globalization as it is practiced today

- Ensuring that a level playing field especially vis-à-vis China is given to American companies by imposing an environmental penalty and a subsidy tax amongst others

- Investing in R&D and pure sciences, which open up avenues for fresh wealth generation

- Investing in Education to turn out more engineers and scientists that can contribute to the development of pure science, technology and manufacturing

- Espousing capitalism and establishing regulatory bodies to curb its excesses

- Realizing that the Chinese game of bureaucratic barriers, large-scale theft, dishonest courts not only void the benefits of globalization but pose a real and existential threat to the US going forward

- Encouraging manufacturing at home by giving subsidized power and other utilities, cutting red tape, providing world-class infrastructure and tax breaks to American companies

By doing all this, I believe that US manufacturing can compete successfully and give the Chinese a run for their money. If Xi Jinping complains like he did when he was exhorting the world to 'say no to protectionism' in an oblique reference to Trump's tariffs on Chinese imports, let him. It's standard Chinese pressure tactics, and it's time to call Xi's bluff.[132]

The only area where I have let go is wages. However, even if Chinese wages are low, in most sectors the increased automation and robotics that American companies can bring to the fore will improve both quality and efficiency thereby significantly denting any competitive edge the Chinese company enjoys due to low labor costs. I will, though, admit that there may still be a few labor-intensive industries like say textiles wherein automation is difficult, and this competitive advantage of low wages can't be eliminated entirely, and thus US companies will continue to remain at a disadvantage. However, I state as follows; such industry sectors are few and far between and are generally low-tech ones wherein wealth generation is also equivalently lesser, and in such cases, I would recommend that the US let things go. If it can achieve the rest, it is more than enough.

In the end, the idea is pretty simple. Manufacturing in America is the sure-fire way to generate enormous wealth, far more than a pure service based economy ever can. Manufacturing will create wealth and jobs, and associated spending on infrastructure will start this positive feedback loop of monies being spent on things that give a return rather than on social responsibilities and debt financing. Manufacturing in America will help avoid the massive trade deficits with China, help America generate wealth to pay off its debt and once again emerge as an economically healthy and vibrant nation.

Good luck and Godspeed.

VIII
For want of a Nail: The Military dimension

Up until now, we've primarily focused on the economic aspects of this sullied relationship between the US and China. In this chapter, I will turn my attention to the military one. I have already given some of the background on the large scale espionage targeting the US defense industry and how China is stealing nearly every military technology available, and even the civilian ones for that matter, from designs of fighter aircraft to nuclear bombs, from smart phones to cars to neutralize America's technological advantage. From this point on, to continue believing in the oft-quoted 'peaceful rise of China' tweet is to live in denial.

China is rapidly building up its military, flush from its trade surpluses and huge foreign reserves and also by applying the cheaper, shortcut way, of stealing designs to manufacture everything from fighters to battleships to missiles. To assume that these are only for self-defense would be naïve. Furthermore, recent years have seen an increase in Chinese posturing, whether it be the bullying of its smaller neighbors in the South China Sea despite an International Court ruling against China's absolute claim to that area, to establishing an Air Defense Identification Zone over the Senkaku Islands claimed by Japan, to attempting a territorial grab of the Doklam plateau in India. Examples abound. The signs are ominous. That China is modernizing its military and does not fear from resorting to bullying its weaker neighbors is a cause for concern.

China is constructing ports in Pakistan and Sri Lanka and taking possession of them on long leases, thereby establishing a toehold in these countries wherein one day it could use them as military bases, say, against India. Another example would be in setting up a naval base in Djibouti giving it strategic access to the throttling point of the horn of Africa through which flows a sizeable proportion of the world's trade.

The final aim of all this is clear; to establish itself as the dominant power in Asia and eventually the world.

Until the 1970s, China had this concept of a 'People's War' that focused on an 'internal struggle'. When that did not work out, as is well known with the fiascos of the Great Leap Forward and the Cultural Revolution, that call to action was modified to 'People's War under modern conditions'[133], which China began implementing in earnest after its opening up to the US in the 1970s.

In this Book, unlike in most other books on this subject, I don't plan on delving deep into China's military spending, the size of its armed forces, its current equipment list etc. It is well known that China is rapidly modernizing its already substantial armed forces and it's no secret that it wants to match and eventually outdo the US, both in quality and quantity. From building tanks, to aircraft carriers to even getting into space warfare with the ability to shoot down satellites, the entire spectrum is covered.

There is a plethora of information already available for those who want to dig deeper. This topic in itself could be the subject matter for a full book. I'm quite sure the reader would have by now come across some newspaper article, TV report, tweet etc., warning about the dangers of China's military buildup. China is increasingly asserting itself, and I do not mean that in a positive way.

In its annual report to the US Congress, comprising no less than 630 pages, the US-China Economic and Security Review Commission warns of a growing arsenal of Chinese weapons. Herein I give the reference of this one report as collated in The National Interest by Harry Kazianis[184], though as I've said one can go as deep as one wants on this subject. Either ways, the conclusion is undeniable. Going forward, the aim of China in current times is no less than establishing itself as the dominant power, initially in Asia, which it probably already is, to eventually in the whole world. For the US, it is not only necessary to ensure economic dominance but equally essential to ensure military dominance if it has to stay on top.

Few would disagree that at present, the US has military superiority in terms of both quality as well as quantity. However, China is slowly and steadily chipping away at this overwhelming dominance. It could be argued that it already is on par as to 'quantity' with large numbers of fighter aircraft, tanks, submarines and such, especially so as it has the largest standing army in the world. However, China is also trying to catch up in quality, something they've historically been poor at.

In the remainder of this chapter, I will give specific examples of how the US can counter the Chinese military threat. Of course, before I get into that, I will again ask the reader to take that veil off the 'peaceful rise' baloney. In essence, what I will be arguing is that in dealing with China, our whole attitude would have to be far more à la Churchill while it is currently far more à la Chamberlain.

The first step in countering China, and this may sound counter intuitive, is to strengthen America's civilian industry. Only when you have a robust industrial base can you divert part of its output to military use. High tech equipment used for military purposes is made up of individual components whose source can eventually be traced back to a non-military civilian origin. Not to mention that basic heavy industries like iron and steel are essential for the construction of battleships, aircraft carriers and tanks. The iron and steel in tanks, the aluminum in fighter planes, all have a civilian origin.

The US first needs a strong civilian base to wean itself off Chinese imports in this twisted game of globalization. The military aspect only strengthens this case. A strong civilian manufacturing base is the foundation for a strong military.

Therefore, all this outsourcing of manufacturing to China is, as argued, not only bad for the US economy but has negative repercussions for America's military capability as well. For example, all equipment bought by the US military has to have a certified US source of origin. However, as was recently pointed out, and I am not surprised, considering the civilian industry in the US has been largely outsourced, that many of the parts of the latest fifth-generation jet fighter, the F-35, were traced to China.[135][136] I wouldn't be surprised if other US military assets were also found to carry parts with a 'Made in China' label.

Ironic, isn't it? Americans are making their best military hardware from products and parts, quite a few of which have been sourced from the PRC. Embarrassing to say the least, and in fact, outright dangerous.

Imagine a worst-case scenario wherein war breaks out between the US and China. Both countries end up imposing trade sanctions on the other. What does the US export to China that the Chinese will miss? Precious little other than mainly agricultural produce that, mind you, the Chinese can grow in-house or import from elsewhere. What will the Americans miss? Firstly, all those civilian goods that US consumes need on a daily basis would be off the shelves and more specifically, for this discussion, the US military would be left without the parts it needs to assemble and service its fighters and other weapon systems.

Sanctions, if imposed by China today, will not only cause hardship to American civilians, but also affect US defense contractors. All those parts or sub-parts that go into some weapon system or another, which were sourced from China, would no longer available. America would carry a wounded pride. Here's your thought for the day, 'Thou cannot win a war against an enemy from whom you source your civilian and ultimately your military equipment'.

However, let's understand that these imports from China are not that big a deal. I mean, given sufficient time, the US industry can easily manufacture what is being currently imported and probably of better quality too. The US may have the technical know-how to make the best steel in the world, but understand this; to do all this overnight when hostilities break out and the flow of goods stops is impossible as it will obviously take time to set up in-house factories. The American military machine, the most powerful military in the world, with the most advanced weapons in the world may well find itself an emperor with no clothes. Reminds me of that saying;

> For want of a nail, the shoe was lost.
> For want of a shoe, the horse was lost.
> For want of a horse, the rider was lost.
> For want of a rider, the message was lost.
> For want of a message, the battle was lost.
> For want of a battle, the kingdom was lost.
> All for want of a horseshoe nail. [187]

Lets us realize that China poses a threat by its ideology and its amassed power, a genuine threat to all free societies on Earth. I claim on similar lines to that of Margaret Thatcher who argued, during the height of the Cold War, that the USSR was an evil empire and that it wasn't enough to just contain it, but it was imperative that it be defeated. Mind you, this new rivalry between the US and China is nothing short of a new Cold War. I will go out on a limb and make this claim that at some time in the future, war between the US and China is inevitable.

Furthermore, this Cold War will be tougher to win than that with the Soviets. With the USSR, the rivalry was only military. The Soviet Union tried to match the US bullet for bullet, fighter for fighter, and failed. The reason being that the economy of the USSR, following the socialist model, was not going to be a match for capitalist USA. All that was required was to be patient until the failed economy of the USSR could not keep up with the US in military spending. In the case of China, though, the fight is on both fronts, economic and military, and the way things stand today it is the US economy that is failing, and it is the Chinese who are going from strength to strength. The US is truly on the ropes.

Thus, the overarching argument is such. Develop your own civilian industrial base, not only as argued to generate wealth in-house, but to enable the use of that as a launching pad to make the best and most advanced weapons in the world. We keep coming back to this idea, which, to reiterate, remains the central idea of this Book; manufacture in-house.

Coming to geo-politics, let us get to some of the specific examples of how China is playing its unscrupulous game on the international stage and how the US can counter it.

Let's take the example of North Korea first.

The North Korean regime is a communist dictatorship and that, too, a hereditary one. A first for a communist state in history. It is probably one of the most draconian regimes to ever exist. It does not brook any dissent. It keeps a watchful eye on its citizens and totally cuts them off from the outside world so that they cannot compare their abject poverty and squalor with living standards elsewhere, especially with their brethren just south of the border. There is no private enterprise, and State-run institutions fail miserably at providing for even the most basic of necessities, like food and healthcare. A failure of the annual rainfall is sure to cause widespread famine, which, in prior years, have led to millions of deaths Those who did survive have had their health severely compromised by malnutrition with the problem being especially bad for children. Their growth both physical and mental is so stunted that they most likely will not be able to function as competent human beings later on in life. Horror stories abound wherein parents have been reported to kill their own children for food.[138] North Korea is an extreme example of a socialist regime that doesn't mind starving its own people to cling onto an outdated idea.[139]

I watched a television documentary once wherein a group of Western surgeons went to North Korea to perform cataract operations. That such a relatively simple surgery could not be done in-house speaks volumes of the shoddy infrastructure and lack of basic healthcare. I was amazed to note that there was not even anesthetic available at these hospitals. Quite obviously, many North Koreans are going blind in later years, as they cannot even have a simple cataract performed on them.

To make things worse, the real horrors are in store for those who speak against the regime. Political prisoners are incarcerated in Concentration camps wherein they are subject to unspeakable torture. There have been reports of prisoners forced to do extreme manual labor without adequate food. Beheadings as punishment are common. There are reports of babies being burned alive as retributive justice for dissenting parents and of widespread rape of female inmates. In many cases, even the extended families of those dissenting are not spared. It is well known amongst North Koreans that if you defect to the South, your family that is left behind will suffer. [140][141]

Coming to the role played by the US, I daresay a survey of the so-called experts and critics will point fingers at the US for this Korean mess. Many criticize US foreign policy for treating North Korea as a pariah state rather than as an equal and responsible member of the international community. Their common aphorism is something like 'Talk with the North, hold dialogue and lift sanctions'.

The North Korean regime is not interested in holding dialogue as peace would bring eventual joining up with the world, making its propaganda fed people realize the truth, which will most certainly result in the collapse of the regime, similar to what happened with East Germany and to the rest of the Soviet Union. Something so obvious is somehow missed by these experts. No, North Korea does not want peace and neither does it want an opening up with the West. Similarly, lifting sanctions won't work as it will only enrich the regime, as the corrupt will siphon off the majority of funds with little, if any, reaching the poor. Furthermore, understand that the North won't give up its nuclear weapons as they remain its one insurance against invasion, as otherwise, its military doesn't stand a chance against the far better equipped South. The great North Korean famine led to mass scale starvation, and yet all the Dear Leader wants to do is build the Bomb. Why, do you think?

To the critics of the US, I cannot understand your silence on the North's draconian regime that would make Dante's hell seem like paradise. Realize this; the very existence of such a regime as that of North Korea, in these times, is deeply unethical, and it is the moral responsibility of all nations and of all citizens of the world, and not just of the US, to free its people. Whatever supposed foreign policy failings of the US, let not the critics, let us all not ever forget this. That, until now, the world has not united and done something to end this barbaric rule is morally inexcusable.

To take this argument further, if doing nothing is inexcusable, I ask what can doing something to support the regime be labeled as?

Enter China. That one of the prime reasons the North Korean regime has been able to last this long is because of support, both economic and military provided by China. In essence, the credit to keep this evil dictatorship propped up goes to them. The purported reason given is that if the regime collapses, China, which is across the border, will be flooded with North Korean refugees.

This cold logic doesn't impress me much. For one, refugees flowing into South Korea would be far higher, and that country isn't complaining. In the event of any such collapse, I would bet good money on South Korea being the preferred destination for migration and further that South

Korea will indeed open its borders and that at the same time China will seal them off.

When Germany was unified, there was concern, along similar lines, of East German refugees flooding into the West. To a certain extent, that did happen. However, most would agree that Germany handled those issues admirably and is a stable and prosperous European powerhouse today.

Let's also consider that China is a far bigger country, with a far greater population, and can conceivably handle refugees, even those who do manage to cross the closed border. Let's not forget that much bigger human displacements and sufferings have been meted out by the CCP on its own citizens, a prime example being the Great Leap Forward. Thus, its argument to keep a despotic regime going to avoid, by Chinese standards, a minor refugee problem doesn't quite ring true.

The reason that China wants to keep the North Korean regime propped up is because it acts as a counterweight to South Korea, which is a US ally, the cost in human suffering be damned. North Korea, in the Chinese mindset, would act as a counterweight to the US-allied South. At first glance, it does seem like standard diplomatic push-pull. However, let's compare the two Koreas.

I have already touched on the brutalities perpetrated by the North Korean regime. Let's get to South Korea. It's a developed country, having a functioning democracy and a free market economy that encourages innovation and is home to world-renowned brands like Samsung, LG, Hyundai, etc. South Korea is a developed nation, and South

Koreans enjoy a high standard of living. The difference between these two countries is like day and night.

The contrast couldn't be starker between the country the US supports and the one that China supports. Critics, take note. At first glance it would seem to be a game of diplomatic brinkmanship, but looking at the horrific conditions of North Koreans, a sense of outrage should well up at some stage.

What is even worse is that China is helping North Korea with missile technology and nuclear expertise that will allow it to build nuclear weapons and hurl one over to South Korea, Japan and eventually onto the US. Imagine the dare. China has openly challenged the world and specifically the US with its nuclear arming of North Korea. By doing so, it has profoundly changed the balance of power in the Korean Peninsula. This is in violation of many international treaties, but the UN and the US have done precious little to punish China. Talk about Bush's 'Axis of Evil'. Rather than North Korea, I daresay, it should have featured China. A few references for the reader:

"Chinese company 'sold North Korea nuclear bomb materials'"
The Independent[142]

"Kim Jong Un's rockets are getting an important boost — from China"
Washington Post[143]

"Five ways North Korea gets money to build nuclear weapons"
CNBC[144]

"How North Korea Got Its "Made in China" Nukes"
Huffington Post[145]

"Mileposts on the road to a North Korean missile: China has supplied all the personnel and material needed to put the U.S. in the crosshairs"
The Washington Times[146]

Let me repeat this. China has supplied know-how and materials that will enable North Korea to develop nuclear weapons and missile delivery systems that can hit continental US. Let this sink in. Understand the importance of what is happening. Furthermore, the US administration knows this but has done precious little other than making disgruntled noises in diplomatic circles and, some sanctions thrown at North Korea, and, mind you, nothing against China.

I ask this openly; is this not Cuba? Are not the two situations eerily similar? In the earlier case, it was the former Soviet Union that supplied nuclear ballistic missiles to Cuba. Today, it is China doing the same to North Korea. I will state the obvious conclusion. The US has had a second Cuba, and the one big difference is the reaction of the US to these two similar situations. America hasn't given a more tepid response ever to a crisis, tantamount to ignoring what has happened.

The reader may ask; what should the American response be? Something on these lines. You, that is, China, have made North Korea a nuclear power. I, that is, the US, will make South Korea and Japan, both developed democracies and societies worth preserving, into nuclear powers too. I will supply nuclear and missile technology to these two nations.

This would still be a bare minimum tit for tat response. Many would be sweating at what I have suggested and be wary of the Chinese counter reaction. Again, this just indicates the level to which the US has stooped to pacify China. China can do something and has already done it, but the US cannot give an equivalent response without fear of reprisals and without condemnation from critics who will accuse it of warmongering.

What would the Chinese response be to the supply of nuclear and missile technology by the US to South Korea and Japan? They will, of course, raise a massive stink at this. I say, let them. They may even threaten nuclear retaliation against South Korea, Japan or even the US. I find that a hollow threat, and I will explain why at the end of this chapter.

China is betting on some conflict in the Korean peninsula in which North Korea nukes South Korea or Japan or the US and in turn gets annihilated, but China itself is let off without a scratch. Brilliant plan, I have to admit. Currently, the US would perceive no reason to nuke China, as the connection hasn't been made. Make it. Enlighten the American people and the world at large. Imagine if it was believed that Cuba had developed nuclear weapons on its own accord, a laughable concept, and then nuked the US, and the USSR was let off because that smoking gun, the U-2 spy photographs, weren't available. Let that not happen in this case too. The intelligence is in. Go to the UN, come on national television, literally go to the rooftops and shout it to the American people and the rest of the world.

The American response, in addition to nuclearizing South Korea and Japan, should be more akin to Kennedy, who, by the way, was considered a weakling in his time, but by today's standards would be thought of as a trigger-happy cowboy.

Let the American President come on TV and announce as Kennedy once did (suitably modified):

"

It shall be the policy of this nation to regard any nuclear missile launched from North Korea (Cuba) against any nation in the Western Hemisphere as an attack by the People's Republic of China (USSR) on the United States of America, requiring a full retaliatory response.

"

Do this. This ultimatum will put a lot of sense into the new Chinese President for life, Xi Jinping. Right now, the Chinese are testing American resolve, and the US is found wanting in every respect. So emboldened are they that they risked nuclearizing a vassal state on similar lines to what the Soviets did, despite knowing well enough Kennedy's historical response. What's shocking is that they've gotten away with it.

Moving on, a similar story applies to the other vassal state of China, viz., Pakistan.

It is a well-known fact that China sees India as a threat going forward to its hegemony in Asia. India, also a developing country, though significantly behind China today, could, with its fast-growing economy, emerge as a threat to Chinese dominance in the future. A fast-growing economy of 1.3 billion Chinese consumers can possibly be challenged by another fast-growing economy of 1.2 billion Indian consumers. The US with its stagnant growth, its burgeoning debt, and a comparatively smaller population of 330 million, will probably not be a competitor in the long term, or so the thinking goes. I am not necessarily saying that India will emerge as a military and economic superpower and pose a serious challenge to any projected Chinese global supremacy. India has its own teething problems and as of this writing lags significantly behind China on most economic indicators. The Chinese economy is considerably larger than that of India and to my dismay, India has gone down the path of a service-based economy rather than a manufacturing one, which, as I have argued, is not the ideal recipe to generate wealth.

However, a common sense approach by the Chinese planners will have them conclude that it's best not to take any chances. Therefore, their foreign policy is to contain India and prevent its rise as a potential future economic and military rival. Thus, their support to Pakistan. As the saying goes, 'an enemy's enemy is my friend'.

I'm not going to raise a stink on economic aid or trade concessions given by China to Pakistan, though that aid is substantial. On the contrary, I will focus on China's crafty scheme to, in fact, subvert Pakistan. What China is doing is loaning big sums to Pakistan under its OBOR (One Belt One Road) initiative such that it hopes Pakistan defaults on its interest and loan repayments, allowing for a Chinese takeover of Pakistan's critical assets and possibly allowing it to one day establish military bases there.[147] This economic aid, which could translate later into military bases, should be a serious concern for India.

However, let's put that aside and discuss one other key aspect here. Just like in the North Korean case, in violation of international treaties, China has supplied Pakistan with nuclear know-how and missile technology.

Again, the US and even the Indian government know this but are largely silent. Admittedly, this is more of a Cuba for India than for the US, but still. All through the Clinton years to Bush and Obama, the Chinese have blatantly ignored international norms to nuclearize and weaponize Pakistan. Why the US remained silent on this is, to me, inexplicable. Probably all in the name of free trade and granting MFN (Most Favored Nation) status to China that, as I have argued, is in fact counterproductive. A lose-lose situation if there ever was one.

"Why China Helped Countries Like Pakistan, North Korea Build Nuclear Bombs,"
US News[148]

"China, Pakistan, and the Bomb: The Declassified File on U.S. Policy, 1977-1997; National Security Archive Electronic Briefing Book No. 114,"
The National Security Archive[149]

"Who Created Pakistan's Nuclear Arsenal?"

Huffington Post[150]

"China's Nuclear Warning"
The Wall Street Journal[151]

"NUCLEAR ANXIETY: THE KNOW-HOW,"
The New York Times[152]

Furthermore, the Chinese have been blocking India's entry into the NSG (Nuclear Suppliers Group) to prevent it from gaining access to fissile material to be used under UN observation for peaceful purposes like electricity generation while clandestinely supplying Pakistan with the same fissile stuff, but of weapons-grade. To ensure that it remains the dominant nuclear power in the region, a dictatorship has been blocking the entry into the NSG of India, a democracy. The prime excuse put forth by the Chinese is that India is not a signatory to the NPT (Treaty on the Non-Proliferation of Nuclear Weapons). On paper, the claim is legitimate. However, dig a little deeper and the claim unravels as India has a proven track record of non-proliferation while China's record, despite being a signatory, is quite the reverse, with it being the dominant supplier of missile technology and fissile material to both Pakistan and North Korea.

Again, I ask, what should the American response be? As I've been advocating, akin to à la Churchill, somewhat along the following lines:

Firstly, America should raise a huge hue and cry locally and internationally about China's clandestine supply of missile technology and nuclear bomb material to Pakistan and North Korea.

India and the US should form a strategic partnership similar to that between Pakistan and China.

The US should recognize India as a nuclear power.

It should supply India with fissile materials needed for its nuclear weapons program.

It should provide India the technical expertise it has through years of testing, which incidentally, China has stolen.

It should help India build its own missile delivery systems.

In essence, a tit for tat response.

Note that the US can provide India with far more than what China today can provide Pakistan. The big picture is like this. China is betting on India and Pakistan fighting a nuclear war in which they end up destroying each other with Pakistan doing so with Made in China nukes and missiles. China is then left as the sole remaining power in Asia and the US looses an important ally.

The standard disclaimer is apposite here. I am an Indian citizen and, though, I have strived to justify my arguments, there is a conflict of interest in what has been said above.

Such is the level that China has cozied up to Pakistan that it used its veto to block a UN resolution calling for a ban on Masood Azhar, a known terrorist who had planned the 2008 Mumbai attacks that killed 166 people and injured more than 600.[153]

"China again sides with Pakistan, blocks UN move to ban Masood Azhar"
The Economic Times[154]

China's pet project, OBOR (One Belt One Road), which aims to boost infrastructure and connectivity by a massive construction program of highways and ports along the historical silk route, is an attempt by China to ensure a hegemony for its goods across the Eurasian countries. Part of the project, specifically the CPEC (China Pakistan Economic Corridor), involves construction of a highway through what is disputed territory between India and Pakistan, viz. Kashmir. That China has the audacity to construct its roads through the Kashmir area controlled by Pakistan, despite India's vehement opposition, should be a cause for worry. It shows that it can even bully a big neighbor and not just its smaller neighbors as in the South China Sea dispute (coming to that soon).

"Opposed to China's CPEC that passes through PoK, India boycotts Belt and Road initiative"
India Today[155]

Let's get to the dispute of the South China Sea or as should be equivalently referred to as the West Philippine Sea. That's another example where blatant Chinese muscle flexing is apparent.

The sea around South East Asia and to the South of China, known, unfortunately, as the South China Sea, is home to many islands which are rich in natural resources. The islands are roughly equidistant from countries such as the Philippines, Vietnam, Malaysia, Brunei, Indonesia, and

China. These islands are disputed in that multiple nations have laid claim to them. However, China being the dominant power is muscling its way in and winning the battle one island at a time. China has already occupied many of the islands and has built military bases, ignoring protests from its weaker neighbors, the United States, and calls from the world community at large to maintain the status quo.[156][157][158][159]

It should be noted that this matter was also arbitrated in the International Court of Justice (ICJ) at The Hague, Netherlands and the judgment went against China in which the Court unanimously found against China's absolute claim of the islands.[160] China, unsurprisingly so, has decided to ignore the judgment and instead has criticized the ICJ.

China is claiming the whole of the South China Sea as its backyard, ignoring protests from competitive claimants like Vietnam, Malaysia, Philippines, Brunei and Indonesia that have overlapping maritime boundaries. But might is right, and the way China has gone about building artificial islands, installing military hardware on them, denying other countries' navies from plying near there, and use of force to ram ships is a classic case of Beijing's in your face bullying.

What should the American response be to this classic case of land/sea grab? Before I go into that, I want to call upon all other countries in the world, especially the parties to this dispute, to stand up to China. The US alone cannot do much here. I call upon the countries of the South China Sea dispute that is, Philippines, Indonesia, Malaysia, and Vietnam to ally with the US. The response to China should be such. The US should take a contract from these nations to create its own artificial islands and build military bases on them just like the Chinese. The islands will remain the property of the claimant nation, that is, the country giving out the contract but the US, will, on their behalf, considering that they do not have the military muscle to do so themselves, set up military bases with some working agreement on what the chain of command should be. China is occupying the islands and building bases. The other countries should do so too, and the US can step in with know-how and equipment.

To reiterate, if China can build islands in disputed territory, so can the Philippines and Vietnam. The reasons they are not are due to economic constraints, limited technological know-how, and a rationed military budget. To reiterate, the US should provide the know-how and the money and get a contract from them to build these bases. It will station weapons on these islands just like the Chinese have done, and some sort of a joint defense agreement can be worked out in which the US will come to the aid of these nations lest China launch an attack.

One may call this warmongering. So be it. As I have articulated throughout this chapter, the military response to Chinese bullying should be of the à la Churchill type. If China can ignore the law of the sea, if it can ignore the claims of other nations, if it can ignore the ruling of the ICJ, then don't complain when other countries, supported by the US, do the same.

Furthermore, cases of China's bullying include the unilateral imposition of an Air Defense Identification Zone over the Senkaku islands, Chinese troop incursions at the tri-junction border between Bhutan, China and India at Dokhlam, the constant harassment of the navies of other nations plying through the international waters of the South China Sea and the Taiwan Straits. Chinese aggression is omnipresent and has to be countered.

China poses a threat not only to the US and to the countries on the South China Sea dispute but also to India, Japan, South Korea and, if a democratic value system is included, a threat to Australia, New Zealand, Canada, Europe and all free societies in the world. China's best allies are North Korea, Pakistan, Nicolás Maduro of Venezuela (its de facto Dictator, who has led his nation to economic ruin) and in the same vein the erstwhile Mugabe of Zimbabwe.

As the saying goes, you are known by the company you keep.

The view of Margaret Thatcher and Ronald Reagan during the height of the Cold War was that the Soviet Union was an evil empire and that it was necessary to not just contain it but to defeat it. To quote her, the Soviet Union represented a "dictatorship of patient, far-sighted determined men...bent on world dominance...and acquiring the means to become the most powerful imperial nation the world has seen."[161]

A similar quote is applicable in this case.

The US may have its flaws, but remains the bulwark of democracy, and it is worthwhile to note that all of those countries that allied themselves with the US have prospered immeasurably more than those countries allied to the former Soviet Union or those countries that remained non-aligned or those that are today allying themselves with China. You probably won't find such a superpower, like the US, in the annals of human history that is so much more powerful than the next in line but has mostly worked as a free and fair global policeman without getting into the excess of empire or of loot or of subjugation.

Coming back to what the standard US response should be to the growing Chinese threat. Specific suggestions with respect to North Korea, Pakistan, and the South China Sea have been given, and I keep hollering on a policy that is more à la Churchill than the current one that is far more à la Chamberlain. However, I would like to sound this caveat: Be prepared that this posturing from both sides could one day lead to a skirmish or an incident in which there is live firing, with probably some loss of life. There is always this risk of posturing turning into a brawl. Critics could seize this as proof of the fallacy of my arguments. However, I will state this; this is a risk that has to be taken. Otherwise, it will be just giving in to China's demands at every stage.

Some will worry whether this small skirmish will turn into a full-blown war. Not likely, but let's entertain every possibility here. If it does so today, then let's understand that the US has far superior conventional forces than the Chinese. It will be a hard fought battle, many lives will be lost on both sides, but the victor is clear. It will be the United States of America. What's more, the Chinese know this and thus they will not escalate a conflict that they are sure to lose but rather prefer to postpone it to a day when they are much stronger and America equivalently weaker.

The reason I bring this forth is twofold. It is not to advocate war but to first demonstrate that the US is far superior conventionally today. The second reason is to bring out the nuclear angle.

The losing side, that is, China will eventually play the nuclear card. It will threaten nuclear retaliation against the US if it does not, say, accept an immediate cessation of hostilities and a return to the old status quo.

Let's talk more about this nuclear blackmail. Any potential conflict scenarios between the US and China will necessarily at some stage have to figure this one out. Should the US keep backing off to Chinese aggression, time and time again, because it does not want to start a conflict, which, if it turns into a full-blown war, may go nuclear?

The answer should be an unequivocal no. Just because the Chinese have the bomb doesn't mean that the US should keep backing off. The obvious question will be: How to deal with this eventuality?

The answer is two-fold.

A similar problem has been faced by India in relation to Pakistan. The sequence is generally such. Pakistani sponsored militants will enter India and commit some act of terrorism. Lives will be lost. There will be a huge hue and cry and Indians, naturally, will demand revenge. The Indian government then threatens Pakistan and gives it an ultimatum to dismantle its terror infrastructure and bring the known terrorists to book else, there could be war. Pakistan does precious little to bring the terrorists to book. Many times the Indian military is given the order to mobilize.

When India threatens military action, Pakistan, knowing that its military is far weaker, invariably uses the nuclear card.

Some statement to that effect is released from the Pakistani government threatening the use of nuclear weapons in the case of War and India eventually backs down. That's the problem with the bomb. The weaker adversary can retaliate with the Nuclear-word, even if it is just used as a threat, and the stronger adversary generally backs down. Of course, if there is an actual conflict, the weaker adversary knows full-well that though it can inflict unacceptable losses on the stronger foe by using nuclear weapons, it will also end up being annihilated. Pakistan figures, and correctly so that the stronger adversary, India, will stand down considering that it has more to lose. This strategy of Pakistan counts on India exercising restraint. India eventually deescalates and everything goes back to normal until the next terror incident.

In the event of a US-China skirmish, with China threatening a nuclear attack, will the US find itself in a similar India-like situation? The answer, thankfully for the US, is no. I'll explain why.

As I have argued, it is the weaker adversary that generally threatens nuclear annihilation first and the stronger foe, having more to lose, that backs off. Herein lies the rub. Today the US is definitely the stronger adversary, something even the Chinese leadership will grudgingly accept. However, one-day China sees itself as being the stronger power. This is where things differ from the India-Pakistan equation. Pakistan does not foresee that it will be stronger than India, ever.

The mindset of the Chinese leaders is such. From their perspective, China will one day undoubtedly emerge as the stronger power, both economically and militarily. It's just a matter of time. It pains me to admit, but I somewhat agree with this assessment and hence the raison d'être for this Book. We could one day have an era of Pax Red China.

Thus, in a sense, if not as facts on the ground, but in the minds of the Chinese leadership, and that's where it really matters anyways, China is the more powerful adversary already. If both, the USA and China, were to annihilate each other in a nuclear holocaust, the Chinese leaders feel, and it's tragic that there is some truth in this argument that they have more to lose. To their minds, the US is already a has-been power. Just a matter of time. Thus, they are not going to risk total destruction before they have had their day in the sun. Think about this. To the Chinese, it's their future, and therefore, according to them, they have more to lose by MAD (Mutually Assured Destruction) than a declining US.

Dear readers, that's the brainwave. That's how the response should be. I repeat, and it pains me to say this, but the US is the Pakistan in this equation, especially in the minds of the Chinese leadership. Thus, the US should not bother so much about facing Chinese nukes. It should instead count on beads of sweat forming on the Chinese leaders' heads that they have to face American nukes.

To the US, I say this: If push comes to shove, do not step back, and if the Chinese invoke the bomb, call their bluff with a reverse threat. I guarantee it will work for the aforesaid reasons. Reply with MAD.

The Chinese don't want their own country destroyed before they have had their day in the sun. They have waited since the end of the last great Chinese empire, probably more than a millennium ago, for this moment in time. They will not allow it to come to a premature end.

Coming to the second part of my answer on nuclear blackmail. There is one clear option when it comes to dealing with the Chinese nuclear threat or for that matter any nuclear threat from any country. The answer is to use technology to safeguard American shores from such a missile attack. Whether the threat originates from the People's Republic of China itself, or as has been discussed earlier, from its allies like North Korea or even, say, from Iran or Russia.

The answer is straightforward. I call upon the US to develop the technology to shoot down these nuclear tipped missiles before they enter American airspace and threaten American cities. Thus, I call upon the US to:

Renew Star Wars or what's formally been known as the SDI (Strategic Defense Initiative).

Any missile fired against the US will be shot down before it enters American airspace. How it is done, whether by firing counter missiles that impact on the incoming missile or by using lasers or some other method, from the ground or from space, I leave that to the scientists and engineers.

The US has the best talent in the world and a penchant for developing the latest in technology. Furthermore, whatever the costs, they are justified. Understand that this is positive spending, on wealth generating avenues. Let me explain. Unlike the trillions spent on the futile Gulf wars, this spending will have a direct salubrious effect on the security of the American nation, safeguarding its wealth, its assets and lives. Even if America ends up spending up to a trillion dollars on this program, it will still be cheaper than the Gulf wars. However, the return, in this case, will be orders of magnitude higher. In fact, I will argue that by promoting a sense of security, as America will now be invulnerable to nuclear attack, it will indirectly generate wealth more than the amount that it ends up spending. The US will be seen as the safest destination, not just from an economic perspective, but even from a military one to park money in. It will secure the US from adversaries that, without mincing words, want to destroy the American nation, kill its people, its values, its way of life and everything I hold dear.

Thus, I call upon the US to restart the Star Wars program. Remember that even the psychological impact the earlier program, as envisaged by Reagan, before it was scrapped by Bill Clinton, had on the Soviet Union was such that it led to an unsustainable arms race for the Soviets, leading to its eventual collapse.

Restart Star Wars. See the massive psychological, military and eventually economic advantage it gives to the US. Economic as in it would make the US more risk-free, thus reducing the rate of borrowing capital and inspiring greater confidence in the everlasting existence of the American nation.

Thus, I ask the reader to take that veil off China's 'peaceful rise' baloney. In dealing with China, our whole attitude would have to be far more à la Churchill while it is currently far more à la Chamberlain. I'm supremely confident that the US can challenge China and beat it at its own game, be it in the economic sphere or, as argued in this chapter, in the military.

Again, good luck and Godspeed.

IX
The other supposedly unrelated Big Two

In this chapter, I will be discussing the two other major problems facing the US, and pretty much, the whole world; that of Islamic terrorism and Global Warming.

The reader could claim, and to a certain extent justifiably so, that these two problems do not fall under the ambit of this Book. Here, we are dealing with the dynamics of the relationship between the US and China, and how China is using every trick in the book to come out on top.

I partly agree.

However, I say this; though the problem of terrorism and global warming does not strictly have a China focus, part of the narrative of this Book is on 'Rebooting America', and it would be remiss of me not to have included these big two. As one of the core messages of the Book is to uphold the US narrative, this discussion will go a long way in making that narrative more relevant.

It may surprise the reader, and I know it did to me, when I initially came up with the idea that although these two problems seem so very different and disparate, they have a similar and sort of an overlapping solution. You may ask: What do global warming and terrorism have in common? Very little, on first thoughts. However, and surprisingly so, it will be argued that the solution proffered for one will automatically help mitigate the other. Thus, the US, or the rest of the world for that matter, does not have to deal with two independent problems. It finally reduces to the classic case of killing two birds with one stone.

The elegant solution offered here is an added reason for incorporating this chapter. In the current political climate in the US, global warming has been put on a back burner with improving the economy, dealing with China and terrorism given more weight, at least by the Trump administration. Here, I try and link the two issues of global warming and terrorism, which should help in marshaling resources and political will to tackle them both.

Before I elaborate on a solution, a quick note to the deniers of global warming and/or terrorism.

One of the arguments against terrorism in the name of Islam is that the Koran does not advocate violence or that Islam is a religion of peace. I am not going to be dragged into a religious debate here of examining the Koran and coming up with verses that promote peace or vice versa and then argue the point. No, not in this Book. However, it is on my to-do lists to write a book that explores the causes of fundamentalism and terrorism at a later date. However, what cannot be denied is that some Muslims, and mind you, not all, are using their religion and a reading of the Koran, however incorrectly per mainstream thought, to kill and maim innocents and non-combatants. That much cannot be denied. That not all Muslims are terrorists is a given and a much trumpeted argument. In fact, I believe the majority to be quite peaceful. However, it cannot be denied that terrorist attacks by Muslims have taken place, '9/11', of course, being the most infamous of these examples, and that there is a significant number of Muslims, even if in a minority, who advocate violence against civilians as a means to an end.

The other issue is that of global warming. Before we tackle the issue, let's first understand the underlying science. CO_2 (Carbon dioxide), along with methane and some other molecules, are what are called greenhouse gases. The science is such. The sun's rays hit the Earth, and some of that energy is trapped by these gases. This trapped energy heats the planet.

That's not necessarily a bad thing. It is this trapped heat of the sun, by these gases, that make the Earth livable. The CO_2 absorbs some of the sun's rays and heats the planet rather than just reflecting sunlight straight back into space. The moon, our neighbor, which is near equidistant from the sun but has no atmosphere and thus no atmospheric greenhouse effect, has a temperature close to minus 170 degree Celsius, a temperature at which, as should be clear, no life can exist. Thus, although painted as a villain, what should be realized first is that these greenhouse gases are essential for life as they help maintain a warm and cozy living habitat. However, as the saying goes, there can be too much of a good thing. If you add more CO2 to the atmosphere, it will trap in more of the sun's energy and warm the planet by that much more.

For example, Venus, which has far higher concentrations of CO2, is sizzling at a temperature of 460 degrees Celsius, hot enough to melt lead. Take note that these high temperatures are because of the CO2 and not so much because of its proximity to the Sun as outer space, in the vicinity of Venus, again has temperatures much below zero Celsius. This much is well-established science. A note to the deniers; no doubts regarding this.

Again, what is not in any doubt is that human activity has been dumping more and more CO2 into the atmosphere, and the concentration of CO2, measured over the past several decades, has been steadily increasing. Again, this has been measured, and there can be no doubt here. Thus, the basic science is clear; the more the CO2, the more the heat of the sun that is trapped and the higher the temperature. There are no two ways about that.

The only plausible disagreement and what the deniers can claim to is the 'when'. When will that day come when CO2 increase in the atmosphere will cross a Rubicon from where we may have a runaway thermal event with the consequent rise in temperatures causing a dramatic shift in the Earth's climate to a level which could make life difficult or non sustainable? The deniers can realistically state that that particular day is far, far away. It cannot be that CO2 keeps rising indefinitely and there is no impact on the Earth's climate. That's just plain wrong.

The debate exists on that one issue. How much time do we have? Scientists have to model a complex system; the climate of the entire planet to get an answer. With so many parameters, non-linearities and unstable equilibriums, even the best models can only give a rough estimate. That's all the deniers can lay claim to. An uncertainty as to the time frame. But not the inevitability of the outcome, if things continue as they do.

Therefore, the grey area is only when our climate will go for a toss. Whether it will be today, tomorrow, next week, month, year, decade, century, millennium or more from now. If nothing is done, eventually that day will come when we see drastic changes to our climate. CO_2 cannot go on increasing indefinitely while at the same time our planet continues to maintain its life-sustaining temperature ranges. That's not possible. By most estimates, those born today, say, in the year 2018, will see drastic effects of climate change by the time they live out an average human lifespan of about 75 years.

Therefore, I call on Americans, let's resolutely deal with all of these problems. The problem of China, the environment and terrorism.

Let me start with terrorism first.

By me, the core and overarching cause of Islamic terrorism can be understood from the simple adage 'An idle mind is the devil's workshop'. Too much free time, lots of money and with nothing much to do.

It could be argued that there are other causes such as some local Mullah brainwashing innocent teens in a

Madrasa, the unresolved Palestinian issue and such. Again, let it be made clear that even if we accept these reasons as a cause, no matter what, no reason can justify terrorism. However, I will stick to my core argument of what ails the Middle East today viz., too much money and too little to do. As a corollary, the Middle Eastern countries have some of the highest percentage of obese people in the world.[162]

It could be argued that my point of view is rather simplistic. I can admit other reasons, but I will stick to this basic claim as being one of the main ones. This topic of terrorism and its causes is exhaustive and will need a dedicated book to explore in detail. The reader may find my logic naïve, as I have not presented any serious argument to support my hypotheses.

With that said, let me put across one.

The spike in terrorism over the past hundred years can be correlated with the rise in the price of oil and the increase in wealth in the Middle East. This one fact stands above all.

A hundred years ago, the phrase Islamic terrorism probably meant nothing. The oil-rich nations of the Middle East were, well, not rich. In fact, they could be classified as one of the most backward and most impoverished areas on this planet. Could there be some relation between an increase in terrorist activity and an increase in prosperity due to the discovery of crude in that region. I firmly believe that if data were mined, statisticians would find a strong correlation between oil riches and terrorism. Whether that correlation is also a causation is something, as stated, I won't delve into in this Book. It's a good subject, maybe, for later.

America has an insatiable appetite for fossil fuels. Coincidence has it that most of this stuff can be found in an area of the Middle East with a preponderance of Islamic nations having majority Muslim populations. The Middle East is rolling in petrodollars. The Arab Sheikhs lead a lavish lifestyle. There is no real need to study, get a degree, work or engage the body or the mind in any productive activity. Nothing in the name of a good day's hard work. What this has resulted is in a feeling of entitlement with no avenues to have good clean fun. No cinemas, no nightclubs, no bars, no discos, what with an imposition of a strict Islamic code. Which is why, as indicated earlier, the Middle East has some of the highest rates of obesity in the world. Nothing to do but go the mall and eat junk food. A sick body and a bored and un-stimulated mind.

It's not much of a stretch to assume that some of these bored youth get carried away by the fiery speeches and anti-western vitriol of some local mullah. Consequently, the mind is corrupted more and more by fundamentalist ideas until the time comes when that young man is willing to wear a suicide belt and blow himself up.

Thus, one of the sure-fire ways to curb the menace of terrorism is for America to stop buying Middle East oil. This is an obvious solution, and I'll admit, I'm not the first to come up with it. Stop the flow of petrodollars and the economies of these countries will be forced to reform. The governments of the Middle East, most of which are hereditary monarchies or theocracies, will be forced to grant freedoms and the people of these countries will be forced to roll up their sleeves and get a good day's job in. I state that eventually terrorism will die out.

Turn off the spigot of petrodollars. Not only would that curb terrorism but will also save the US billions of dollars in imports. Furthermore, as has been argued earlier, these oil exports are not 'free trade' in the true capitalist way. OPEC is a cartel, a monopoly. I have spoken against this form of capitalism. The US importing oil does not fall into, as I have argued, beneficial globalization.

However, the problem, as many would argue, is with its implementation. The obvious query would be; where would the gas we tank up in our cars would come from? I'll come to that soon.

Before I get to where the US can source its oil from, let me come to a similar situation vis-à-vis the EU (which in this context would include the UK) and Russia. Firstly, I'm not saying that Russia is a state sponsorer of terrorism. However, the Russia of today under Putin is most definitely anti-American and anti-West in general. It all started well with the fall of the Berlin Wall and then under Gorbachev/ Yeltsin. It would have seemed that Russia and the West would completely bury the hatchet and form a friendship based on shared values of freedoms and democracy that I'm guessing Yeltsin wanted for his people. Russia would have finally integrated with Europe. Under Putin, those dreams are pretty much over. Putin with his endless terms as President is concentrating power with him and seems more and more like a Dictator. Russia is becoming a totalitarian State with Putin at the helm. The opposition has been systematically weakened and eliminated even, and criticism of Putin can lead you to jail.

Today's Russia is not an innovation hub, is not business friendly, has endemic corruption and has monopolies controlled by oligarchs. However, it must be said that under Putin, the standards of living of the Russian people have gone up significantly. Why? The simple answer is natural resources, chief amongst them being oil and gas. Russia has vast deposits of natural gas. Again, a similar argument applies here. If you want serious reforms from Russia, if you want its government to respect its citizen's rights, if you don't want to hand over monies to a country that is a serious threat to American and European security, has already annexed Crimea and aids a civil war in the east of Ukraine, the EU must stop buying oil and gas from Gazprom.

What is the alternative to importing crude from Russia or the Middle East? The US, and also the EU, though I will stick to the US here, can source its oil and gas from within its own territories. This, as the reader would have guessed, is similar to what I have argued in the case of manufacturing.

Sounds impossible, many would say. The US does not have significant crude reserves. That would be right. However, it has vast resources of Shale and clathrate hydrates from which oil can be extracted.

A caveat is needed here. The temporary answer here is shale, and as I will propound in the next section on global warming, the permanent solution is electricity from renewable resources.

Shale is a rock that has organic oil bound within its structure. Clathrates are ice-like solids that have trapped oil within its crystalline structure. The US, and also India, have an abundance of both of these minerals. There is more oil trapped in these two compounds than all the crude in the world. This is a resource just waiting to be exploited.

The good news is that the US has indeed taken to shale extraction in a big way so much so that, and this may sound scarcely believable, US shale production today exceeds Saudi light sweet crude production.[163] However, as these technologies are in their infancy, the cost of production is high, making shale profitable only if crude is above fifty dollars a barrel.

The suggestions are such: The US government should give subsidies, tax breaks and easy loans to its shale manufactures and invest in R&D to make the technology cheaper and more economical. If shale is able to become profitable below 30 dollars, that would be the end of OPEC, and that's a big thing. As stated, I am against trading with a cartel. That's not globalization in its true spirit. Thus, I advocate, if crude falls below 30 dollars per barrel, imposing an anti-dumping duty on crude imports to protect America's local shale manufacturers. The price of OPEC oil is not so much determined by the law of supply and demand on a commodities exchange but by increasing or decreasing crude production by the chip holders, the OPEC countries. Thus, US granting protection to its shale and clathrates extracting businesses is well justified.

The world has accepted the OPEC cartel for way too long. These countries are lucky to have a natural resource but what is not right is that they have monopolized this reserve by forming a cartel and used it to establish a stranglehold on the rest of us. If given the appropriate encouragement, I believe US shale and clathrates manufacturers will even exceed US oil demand and the US can turn into a net exporter. I am willing to bet on American innovation, entrepreneurship and their go-getter attitude over OPEC's largesse anytime. On similar lines, the EU can follow the American lead and wean itself off Gazprom.

America becoming self sufficient and probably even a net exporter of oil will save petrodollars, help reduce the trade deficit, end America's slavish dependence on Gulf oil, encourage industry and innovation in-house and deal a body blow to terrorism.

A win-win, if there ever was one.

Coming to the next big issue facing not just the US but also the whole world, that of global warming. I have already stated my case as to why global warming is real. Increased CO_2 will lead to increased temperatures. No two ways about it. Furthermore, it is well documented that human activity has contributed to this increase as the global concentration of CO_2, seen in the data over the past 50+ years has gone up from 300 to almost 400 ppm (parts per million).[164] The only debate and the only proverbial straw at which the deniers can realistically clutch on to is the timescale. What can be said to be uncertain, as climate modeling is an extremely complicated endeavor, is the timelines involved. When will this continuous increase in CO_2 and the corresponding increase in temperature, lead to destabilizing climate change? Will it be tomorrow or in the next thousand years? My gut instinct tells me that it will be sooner rather than later.

For example, my city of Mumbai, previously known as Bombay, is in the news every monsoon for torrential rains leading to floods. These floods have been a regular occurrence during the monsoons since around 2005. It's become a nightmare to wade through the city's monsoons, with people being stuck as roads and rail tracks get flooded and all transportation grinds to a halt. It's sad for me to say this, but you can see the fear in the eyes of the average resident who when they leave home for work in the morning, during the monsoon season, are worried if they'll be able to make it safely back home at the end of the day. Take a ride on the public transport of Mumbai, say, in the jam-packed trains, and the conversation will mostly be on the weather forecast for the day.

Part of the reason for the water accumulation during heavy rainfall can be blamed on shoddy infrastructure and a negligent city administration. However, this was true even before the regular floods became a norm. In a dubious distinction, Mumbai is being considered for a Guinness book award as having the maximum number of potholes for any city in the world.[165]

I'll go on a limb and say this; I can tell that the amount of rainfall has been increasing through the years in my city. I fully submit to those critics who will say that one person's subjective observations of one particular city cannot be used to draw broad conclusions. I accept. Though I will say that Mumbai, my city, is dying a slow death. You can feel the losing battle the citizens are fighting against the elements.

Monsoons, which were once eagerly awaited to bring relief from the summer heat, are now looked upon with trepidation. With the double whammy of a creaking British era infrastructure not upgraded in the decades since combined with Nature's wrath, I am not optimistic.

To reiterate, let it be understood that although increased CO2 means increased temperatures, it does not mean that all days are going to be hot. The Earth's climate is a complex system, and weather is cyclic. It should be noted that an increase in temperature leads to a more energetic environment. Basic thermodynamics. On average, temperatures will rise, but because of this increase in energy (which should more appropriately be called entropy, to use the correct scientific term), wild fluctuations in weather will also be the norm. Therefore, you can have heat spells followed by cold spells, and the cold spells may be really cold. Nevertheless, understand this: on average temperatures will increase. This increase in atmospheric entropy will give rise to extremes, both in hot and cold. Thus, most days will be hot with a few days very hot and a few days very cold and that it would be wrong to consider a cold spell as proof against an on-average warming.

Now, let's try to come to grips with this issue too.

In the last section, I have advocated the use of shale and clathrates instead of crude. Though this will reduce dependency on crude from the Middle East, it will not solve the problem of global warming as the burning of fossil fuels, obtained through either the shale or crude route, will contribute to greenhouse emissions, most particularly CO2.

Thus, the rise in CO2 because of humankind's activities will continue unabated.

However, at the beginning of this chapter, I hinted that solving one of these problems would help in solving the other. Here's how:

Let's come to why we need gasoline or other fossil fuels. The basic answer is that the energy content in these fossil fuels is largely used to drive 'something'. That 'something' invariably is a motor. A motor is a device that keeps rotating, and that rotating motion is transformed into the type of activity we need performed.

For most equipment like, say, pumps, ceiling fans, etc., all that is required is this circular motion to do the job. Keep going round and round, and the needful gets done. However, in cars, for example, this circular motion is transformed into linear forward motion by use of a crankshaft. A similar mechanism exists for trains. For ships, the circular motion of the propellers drives the ship forward. For propeller airplanes, circular motion of the fan blades is transformed into forward thrust. Jet engines, however, use direct explosion of the gasoline mixture to move forward, and I'll come to that at the end.

Most motion is initially rotation. The question is, do we need fossil fuels to generate this rotating motion? The surprising answer is that in most cases, we don't. Electricity is the cheapest and most efficient way of achieving circular motion by use of electric motors. An electric motor is far more efficient than a petrol engine, and electricity is far cheaper. Thus, wherever possible, and the keyword is 'wherever', it would be a no-brainer to use electricity rather than any other energy source to drive your machine. When the equipment undergoing rotation is fixed, like say as a pump, a ceiling fan, or a machine in a factory, it's no problem. Just plug the machine that has the inbuilt motor into an electric socket, and it's done.

The problem arises when the equipment is moving, for example, in an automobile. The issue here is that you can't take that electric socket along with you for the drive. The minute the car moves forward the socket comes unhinged, and the electric supply fails, stopping the motor. Therefore, electric cars carry their own electric supply on board in the form of batteries.

Thus, the key understanding is that when equipment moves, you have to carry your energy source along with it, say, in a battery or as is currently more popular today, gasoline in the tank. Gasoline has been hitherto preferred as it represents the least carrying load for the maximum energy released and thus is the fuel of choice.

To solve the issue of greenhouse emissions, I will split this problem into two parts.

Let's first take those equipments that rotate but are stationary. They represent the largest fraction of rotating equipment and we don't need fossil fuels to make the machine move. As stated, for them, electricity is the cheapest and the most efficient power source. What we have to do, to avoid the specter of warming, is to ensure that in these cases electricity is generated from non fossil fuel sources. The good news is that it's not difficult. To do that we ensure that electricity is not produced by burning naphtha or coal. This in itself will take care of a significant fraction of warming pollution. Generate electricity by using hydropower, wind, solar or nuclear fission and invest in fusion, which, when operational, would give a perennial source of power.

Solar is coming up in a big way with prices of solar panels been reduced to an extent that it will be cheaper to generate electricity through solar rather than by coal around 2020.[166] I am proud to add that India is in the forefront of the solar energy revolution today. It has an installed capacity of 12,000 GWh (gigawatt hours), and with many private players in this industry and consequent competition, it may surprise the reader to know that the price per unit of electricity generated through solar as of this writing is around 20% lower than coal.[167]

Again, this is money well spent. If solar is cheaper than coal, go in for massive solar parks, generate electricity and offer them at free or subsidized rates, as argued, to your industries. You will give a fillip to the industry while at the same time reduce your carbon footprint and reduce your import bill. This is positive spending that will generate electricity cheaply, curb warming pollution and as argued, terrorism, and encourage local industry. Similarly, spend good money on R&D to get the most efficient solar panels, wind turbines and such. Which technology, say wind or solar or nuclear or hydro, will eventually win or will they all coexist, I can't tell. Let a competitive market decide.

Generate electricity from 100% renewable sources, which, as stated, is not that difficult as, for example, soon it will be cheaper to produce electricity from solar than from coal. By doing this, a big chunk of the global warming pollution is taken care off.

Coming to rotating machines that convert their rotation into some kind of motion, most likely translational, such as in cars, planes, trains, and ships. Again, electricity is the most efficient and economical way to power these machines, but the problem lies with a steady supply of electricity. When a plug-in socket is not possible, these vehicles will have to carry their electricity supply onboard. To reiterate, this is where the problem lies of having a good supply of ready electricity on the move. If that problem is solved, no manufacturer will ever go for the more expensive and less efficient gasoline-based engines.

On average, a gasoline engine is only 20% efficient as opposed to an electric motor, which is 90+%.[168] Not to mention, electricity is much cheaper. Taking a big picture point of view, most of the problems with renewable electricity generation and efficient electric motors have been solved.

What has not been resolved is the problem of electricity storage. Batteries of today do a dismal job at it. They are expensive, take long to recharge, and their charge carrying capacity limits the range of electrically driven vehicles.

The current lithium-ion batteries don't have enough oomph and range. Plus, lithium cannot be a lasting solution because there is only so much of it, and even if the batteries are recycled, the resource will deplete over time, and, of course, lithium mining poses an environmental hazard.

However, I believe that the time is ripe to let American innovation out of the bag. As I keep saying, America is at its best when innovating. Pour money into R&D and grants to universities and let private enterprise come up with a solution. Companies are already experimenting with non-metal batteries like polymer gel, Teflon electrolyte, etc., and I'm sure given enough impetus a solution will be found in a battery that can carry a hefty charge and is not dependent on environmentally polluting metals that are anyways rare on this planet.

Once a good battery becomes a reality, it would lead to electric cars that are cheap to manufacture, maintain, exceedingly cheap to the mile, do not contribute to pollution and global warming, cut the dependence of foreign imports for oil and thus solve the problem of global warming and terrorism in one go.

Electric trains run on electricity supplied by overhead wires, which act as a movable socket. They don't have to carry their electricity on-board. Nevertheless, once we have a good battery on which we can run our cars, scaling up that technology to electric ships won't be that hard. What will continue be a bit of a problem is scaling that technology to airplanes. Electric engines powering airplanes may be a tad difficult. However, it may surprise you to know that Airbus has already started with a plan to build an electric passenger jet.[169]

The key issue is to wean away 'moving motors' from fossil fuel by coming up with an efficient battery. Do that and along with the 'nonmoving motors' that already use electricity you have a shot at solving the problem of global warming by eliminating the burning of fossil fuels, provided that electricity so generated is from renewable resources, something entirely within our capacity to do. Already in India, 33% of electricity is generated by renewable resources, and this figure is steadily rising.[170]

What little CO2 is still emitted after this bulk is taken care of can then be easily handled by a CCS (Carbon Capture and Sequestration) type technology, a technology that captures atmospheric carbon and buries it deep underground.

Thus, it would seem hard to believe, but we already have in large part the technology, up and ready, to solve the problems of terrorism and global warming in one go.

All we need is a good battery... Make one, America.

X
Conclusion

I hope this Book has, by now, impressed upon the reader the dangers of what the CCP refers to as the 'peaceful rise of China'.

For America, it is time to choose its destiny going forward. For the rest of the world, there is also a choice. Do we support the US or China, or stay neutral? Furthermore, do we ourselves implement the economic policies outlined herein to ensure our own prosperity and reduce our slavish dependence on Chinese imports?

The choice has to be made now and by everybody. It is still not too late.

A thank you to all who've braved this Book up to this point. It's been a long journey for sure. At times, if I've seemed a bit long-winded, I apologize. The only defense I'll offer up is that I had to do a lot of preparatory groundwork before I could conclude.

This Book in many areas has gone against the popularly accepted narrative. For example, if I were to write a book praising globalization, all I had to do was use clichés like free markets, cheaper goods, mutual prosperity for all and so on. We've all been so bombarded with these one-liners that we've come to believe in them explicitly without thinking them through. To argue against the trend takes much more effort. One has to get to the brass tacks and start from scratch. As I keep saying, the 'why' is more important than the 'how'. By now, I hope to have convinced the reader as to my narrative and if not, at least, sowed a seed of doubt in their mind.

All's said that had to be said. We started with an argument about the economic problems facing the US and then went on to a comparison of the value systems of these two countries. I argued as to why, despite some flaws, the narrative of the US is far superior to that of China, and to that offered by any other country in all of human history.

We went over some basic economics and tried to understand where we've gone off course. I then argued against globalization as practiced in the current context, specifically with respect to Sino-US 'free' trade. From that point on, we moved to the steps that the US can take to counter China, chief amongst them being to reindustrialize and start manufacturing in-house. We then covered the military aspect of why it would be foolish for the US to keep giving in to Chinese expansionist aims and how it should respond to Chinese nuclear proliferation.

Finally, I talked about the other two major issues of today, that of global warming and terrorism, and why they are relevant in the context of this Book. Part of the steps to be taken in 'Rebooting America' would require the US to tackle these two head on. Furthermore, I explain how these two issues are surprisingly not that different from each other and how solving one would help in solving the other.

Before, I conclude, there is one more argument I will make. Bear with me.

There are those who will agree with the conclusions offered up in this Book. They will admit to the dangers of a China-dominated world and that of declining American power. However, they would be unwilling to do anything about it. To them, China has already become the all-powerful and dominant power. The basic core argument offered by them is that the US can no longer live without China. So intertwined are these two nations and so hopelessly dependent has the US become on Chinese imports that normal life in the US would be severely impacted without its trade with China. America would go back to the Stone Age, or so they claim. There is some merit in this argument, but, I can't help but pass this comment that if this was known, why-oh-why did you trade off all your manufacturing away to China in the first place? However, accepting some merit herein, I, therefore, do not advocate an immediate cessation of all trade with China. America should industrialize and as it does so, slowly start weaning itself off Chinese imports.

Let's realize that this hopeless dependence of the US on imported Chinese goods is a new phenomenon. Nixon went to China in 1979 and opened it up to the West. Even after that date, it was several years before Sino-US trade could reach the gargantuan levels it has today. Therefore, to the naysayers who claim that the US cannot survive without China, it has done so from 1776 to 1979. For all of those years, there was hardly any trade between these two countries. Was not the US a developed nation then? Did it not have a high standard of living, especially so since the beginning of the twentieth century? All of that with trading naught with China.

I am not criticizing Nixon for doing what he did. It is difficult to predict the consequences of your actions all these years down the line. The argument then was that by cozying up to China, the US could pull it out of the Soviet orbit, which, by the way, Nixon successfully did. Though not debated as much, this probably helped hasten the fall of the Soviet Union and end the Cold War.

Coming back, let's realize that America was still America before 1979. It was a prosperous country having a high standard of living and had been so for many decades prior. This is the best argument against the naysayers who claim that America cannot exist without China. It has existed so from 1776 to 1979, more than 200 years and quite a few of them as a prosperous nation and as a world leader.

The big question, therefore, is whether or not the US has gained from this move to China in the long run. The answer is a big No. Yes, it did get access to cheap goods but, as has been argued, at the expense of impoverishing itself and destroying its wealth generating capacity. On the other hand, China, from being a basket case economy due in part to the catastrophic disasters of the Cultural Revolution and the Great Leap Forward got to piggyback on America, get rich and reach the heights it has today. China has benefited a million-fold more. The issue I have with this is not so much the prosperity of China, but that it did so with subterfuge and theft, like a leach, and even after all of this, it has the most hostile of intentions towards the US.

I will end this Book in a slightly unconventional way. I will be narrating to you two scenes from two different movies. These movie scenes are obviously fictional. After talking so much on arguments and on facts and data, I thought it best to end on a fictional note. Somewhat of a change. Although the accounts are obviously fictional, I do believe they bring out the essence of these two nations.

Thus, I end this Book with a narration of these two scenes as played out.

The first scene is that from the movie Shanghai Noon, starring Jackie Chan. The stage is set in Beijing, China during the reign of some Emperor sometime in the nineteenth century. Jackie plays the role of one of the Emperor's royal guards. Jackie is to be dispatched to the US to retrieve a runaway princess. The scene is such; he is summoned to the Emperor's palace. In the presence of the Emperor, Jackie immediately falls to the floor on bent knees with his face almost touching the ground in what I can only describe as a turtle position. Imagine his face and torso parallel with the ground, with bent hands and legs. I recommend the reader watch that scene to get a better idea. I would be hard pressed to even get into such an uncomfortable position even if I were to let go of my self-respect. When the Emperor moves, if Jackie has to follow, he has to crawl on all fours to keep up. Crawl... Surprisingly, the message that Jackie wants to convey is not that the viewer should be appalled by this subhuman conduct, but instead, it's meant to demonstrate the positive aspects of total devotion. I am deeply disturbed by that scene. To genuflect to such an extent to authority and that too for someone unelected and as is later revealed, being all of thirteen years old is not done. Of course, China doesn't have an Emperor anymore but, mind you, the CCP is no less exacting, demanding a similar absolute and unquestioning obedience from its subjects.

The other scene is from the movie Lincoln, in which the role of Abraham Lincoln is played by Daniel Day-Lewis. The film is about the Thirteenth Amendment to the US Constitution abolishing slavery and is played out during the time of the American Civil War. Incidentally, the time scale for both the movies is similar, with both of them set in the middle of the nineteenth century. The scene starts with President Lincoln out somewhere amongst his Union troops. Random troops come up to Lincoln and chat with him. I mean, imagine being able to walk up to the President and chitchat. A group of white soldiers comes up, followed by two black soldiers and they chat.

A black man chatting with the President discussing the War, quoting from his one earlier speech, commenting on his wiry hair, joking about his barber, and talking essentially as if the two were equals. No difference in position, class, or status. This is what I love about America.

To the reader, I say, choose...

**If you've found this book useful,
please consider leaving a short
review on Amazon**

References

[1]   G. Colvin, "Study: China Will Overtake the U.S. as World's Largest Economy Before 2030," 9 February 2017. [Online]. Available: http://fortune.com/2017/02/09/study-china-will-overtake-the-u-s-as-worlds-largest-economy-before-2030/.

[2]   W. contributors, "China's peaceful rise," Wikipedia, The Free Encyclopedia., 6 December 2018. [Online]. Available: https://en.wikipedia.org/w/index.php?title=China%27s_peaceful_rise&oldid=87237866.

[3]   M. Winter, "Poll: China, not Iran, now USA's top enemy," USA TODAY, 20 February 2014. [Online]. Available: https://www.usatoday.com/story/news/nation/2014/02/20/china-iran-enemy-gallup-poll/5651915/.

[4]   J. Diamond, "Trump: 'We can't continue to allow China to rape our country'," CNN, 2 May 2016. [Online]. Available: https://edition.cnn.com/2016/05/01/politics/donald-trump-china-rape/index.html.

[5]   "China GDP Annual Growth Rate," Trading Economics, [Online]. Available: https://tradingeconomics.com/china/gdp-growth-annual.

[6]   M. Egan, "2008: Worse than the Great Depression?," CNN Business, 27 August 2014. [Online]. Available: https://money.cnn.com/2014/08/27/news/economy/ben-bernanke-great-depression/index.html.

[7]   J. Blanke and S. Krogstrup, "Negative interest rates: absolutely everything you need to know," World Economic Forum, 2 November 2016. [Online]. Available: https://www.weforum.org/agenda/2016/11/negative-interest-rates-absolutely-everything-you-need-to-know/.

[8]   "US Debt Clock.org," [Online]. Available: http://www.usdebtclock.org/.

[9]   "Trade in Goods with China," United States Census Bureau, [Online]. Available: https://www.census.gov/foreign-trade/balance/c5700.html.

[10]   G. Satell, "Wake up America! This Is The Real Problem With The US Economy," Forbes, 29 October 2016. [Online]. Available: http://www.forbes.com/sites/gregsatell/2016/10/29/wake-up-america-this-is-the-real-problem-with-the-us-economy/#2a63eb261206.

[11]   P. Davidson, "USA's creaking infrastructure holds back economy," USA TODAY, 20 May 2012. [Online]. Available: https://usatoday30.usatoday.com/money/economy/story/2012-05-20/creaking-infrastructure/55096396/1.

[12]   "China Foreign Exchange Reserves," Trading Economics, [Online]. Available: https://tradingeconomics.com/china/foreign-exchange-reserves.

[13]   W. contributors, "Economy of China," Wikipedia, The Free Encyclopedia, 22 December 2018. [Online]. Available:

https://en.wikipedia.org/w/index.php?title=Economy_of_Chin
a&oldid=874864090.

[14]   D. Workman, "Crude Oil Exports by Country," World's Top
        Exports, 30 November 2018. [Online]. Available:
        http://www.worldstopexports.com/worlds-top-oil-exports-
        country/.

[15]   D. Trotta, "Iraq war costs U.S. more than $2 trillion: study,"
        Reuters, 14 March 2013. [Online]. Available:
        https://www.reuters.com/article/us-iraq-war-anniversary-
        idUSBRE92D0PG20130314.

[16]   "How much petroleum does the United States import and
        export?," US Energy Information Administration, [Online].
        Available: https://www.eia.gov/tools/faqs/faq.php?id=727&t=6.

[17]   W. contributors, "Halabja chemical attack," Wikipedia, The
        Free Encyclopedia., 26 October 2018. [Online]. Available:
        https://en.wikipedia.org/w/index.php?title=Halabja_chemical_
        attack&oldid=865813900.

[18]   A. S. Ahmed and R. Grim, "For The Record, Yes, George
        W. Bush Did Help Create ISIS," HuffPost US, 15 May 2015.
        [Online]. Available: http://www.huffingtonpost.com/entry/jeb-
        bush-isis_n_7284558.html?section=india.

[19]   K. Frayer, "China votes to make Xi Jinping ruler for life," The
        Week, 12 March 2018. [Online]. Available:
        http://www.theweek.co.uk/92214/china-votes-to-make-xi-
        jinping-ruler-for-life.

[20]   "WHen Even the Super Genius MicHio KaKu LOST HiS
        COOL ! ! !," RT, [Online]. Available:
        https://www.youtube.com/watch?v=sdGOrWmVMv8.

[21]   "America's Founding Documents," National Archives,

[Online]. Available:
http://www.archives.gov/exhibits/charters/declaration_transcri
pt.html.

[22]   W. contributors, "United States Bill of Rights," Wikipedia,
The Free Encyclopedia., 20 December 2018. [Online].
Available:
https://en.wikipedia.org/w/index.php?title=United_States_Bill
_of_Rights&oldid=874586153.

[23]   "Early American contributions to democracy," Skwirk,
[Online]. Available: http://www.skwirk.com/p-c_s-1_u-105_t-
279_c-931/nsw/hsie/introduction-to-democracy/democratic-
development/early-american-contributions-to-democracy.

[24]   W. contributors, "French Revolution," Wikipedia, The Free
Encyclopedia., [Online]. Available:
https://en.wikipedia.org/wiki/French_Revolution#Long-
term_impact.

[25]   W. contributors, "Alexis de Tocqueville," Wikipedia, The
Free Encyclopedia., 13 November 2018. [Online]. Available:
https://en.wikipedia.org/w/index.php?title=Alexis_de_Tocque
ville&oldid=868653125.

[26]   W. contributors, "Gettysburg Address," Wikipedia, The Free
Encyclopedia., 19 November 2018. [Online]. Available:
https://en.wikipedia.org/w/index.php?title=Gettysburg_Addres
s&oldid=869579993.

[27]   I. Team, "India has lowest police population ratios in the
world," The Hans India, 29 July 2016. [Online]. Available:
http://www.thehansindia.com/posts/index/National/2016-07-
29/India-has-lowest-police-population-ratios-in-the-
world/245425.

[28] W. contributors, "United States Bill of Rights," Wikipedia,
      The Free Encyclopedia., 20 December 2018. [Online].
      Available:
      https://en.wikipedia.org/w/index.php?title=United_States_Bill
      _of_Rights&oldid=874586153.

[29] W. contributors, "Religion in Saudi Arabia," Wikipedia, The
      Free Encyclopedia., 6 December 2018. [Online]. Available:
      https://en.wikipedia.org/w/index.php?title=Religion_in_Saudi
      _Arabia&oldid=872366920.

[30] H. Agerholm, "Saudi Arabia elected to UN women's rights
      commission," Independent, 24 April 2017. [Online].
      Available: http://www.independent.co.uk/news/world/middle-
      east/saudi-arabia-un-womens-right-commission-un-watch-
      middle-east-muslim-driving-clothes-a7698536.html.

[31] W. contributors, "Falun Gong," Wikipedia, The Free
      Encyclopedia., 23 December 2018. [Online]. Available:
      https://en.wikipedia.org/w/index.php?title=Falun_Gong&oldid
      =875089162.

[32] W. contributors, "Freedom of religion in China," Wikipedia,
      The Free Encyclopedia., 30 December 2018. [Online].
      Available:
      https://en.wikipedia.org/w/index.php?title=Freedom_of_religi
      on_in_China&oldid=875981988.

[33] "scientific method," English Oxford Living Dictionaries,
      [Online]. Available:
      https://en.oxforddictionaries.com/definition/scientific_method
      .

[34] J. R. Benjamin, "Three Words Ben Franklin Crossed out of
      the Declaration of Independence," 8 April 2014. [Online].
      Available: https://jrbenjamin.com/2014/04/08/three-words-

ben-franklin-crossed-out-of-the-declaration-of-independence/.

[35] W. contributors, "Geocentric model," Wikipedia, The Free Encyclopedia., 22 December 2018. [Online]. Available: https://en.wikipedia.org/w/index.php?title=Geocentric_model&oldid=874967579.

[36] J. Dillinger, "Nobel Prize Winners By Country," World Atlas, 7 March 2018. [Online]. Available: http://www.worldatlas.com/articles/top-30-countries-with-nobel-prize-winners.html.

[37] V. Rana, "The Expansion and the Consolidation of the British in India," HistoryDiscussion.net, [Online]. Available: http://www.historydiscussion.net/history-of-india/the-expansion-and-the-consolidation-of-the-british-in-india/2077.

[38] "On French Colonial Expansion," Vancouver Island University, [Online]. Available: https://web.viu.ca/davies/H479B.Imperialism.Nationalism/Ferry.Fr.imperialism.1884.htm.

[39] W. contributors, Wikipedia, The Free Encyclopedia., [Online]. Available: https://en.wikipedia.org/wiki/Economic_history_of_the_United_States#/media/File:GDP_per_person_in_the_United_States.png.

[40] W. contributors, "Emperor of China," Wikipedia, The Free Encyclopedia., 20 December 2018. [Online]. Available: https://en.wikipedia.org/w/index.php?title=Emperor_of_China&oldid=874606952.

[41] "GDP per capita (current US$)," The World Bank, [Online]. Available: https://data.worldbank.org/indicator/NY.GDP.PCAP.CD.

[42] W. contributors, "Deng Xiaoping," Wikiquote, ., 5 September 2018. [Online]. Available: https://en.wikiquote.org/w/index.php?title=Deng_Xiaoping&oldid=2463043.

[43] S. Shan, "Interview: China's Great Famine Years 'Were an Era of Cannibalism'," Radio Free Asia, 22 November 2013. [Online]. Available: http://www.rfa.org/english/news/china/cannibalism-11222013104349.html.

[44] W. contributors, "Great Leap Forward," Wikipedia, The Free Encyclopedia., 24 December 2018. [Online]. Available: https://en.wikipedia.org/w/index.php?title=Great_Leap_Forward&oldid=875167126#Famine_deaths.

[45] W. contributors, "The Holocaust," Wikipedia, The Free Encyclopedia., 31 December 2018. [Online]. Available: https://en.wikipedia.org/w/index.php?title=The_Holocaust&oldid=876110679#Victims_and_death_toll.

[46] "China's Great Famine: the true story," The Guardian, [Online]. Available: https://www.theguardian.com/world/2013/jan/01/china-great-famine-book-tombstone.

[47] W. contributors, "Cultural Revolution," Wikipedia, The Free Encyclopedia., 29 December 2018. [Online]. Available: https://en.wikipedia.org/wiki/Cultural_Revolution.

[48] W. contributors, "Anastasia Lin," Wikipedia, The Free Encyclopedia., 31 August 2018. [Online]. Available: https://en.wikipedia.org/w/index.php?title=Anastasia_Lin&oldid=857481984.

[49] "China: Rise in forced evictions fuelling discontent," Amnesty International, 11 October 2012. [Online]. Available:

https://www.amnesty.org/en/latest/news/2012/10/china-rise-forced-evictions-fuelling-discontent/.

[50]   W. contributors, "Organ harvesting from Falun Gong practitioners in China," Wikipedia, The Free Encyclopedia., 29 December 2018. [Online]. Available: https://en.wikipedia.org/w/index.php?title=Organ_harvesting_from_Falun_Gong_practitioners_in_China&oldid=875918354.

[51]   M. Robertson, "US HOUSE OF REPRESENTATIVES PASSED H.RES 343 UNANIMOUSLY, CONDEMNS ORGAN HARVESTING OF FALUN GONG," Epoch Times, 13 June 2016. [Online]. Available: http://www.stoporganharvesting.org/us-house-of-representatives-passed-h-res-343-unanimously-condemns-organ-harvesting-of-falun-gong/.

[52]   M. Palin, "'A bloody harvest': Thousands of people slaughtered for their organs, new report reveals," News Pty Limited, 28 June 2016. [Online]. Available: https://www.news.com.au/world/asia/a-bloody-harvest-thousands-of-people-slaughtered-for-their-organs-new-report-reveals/news-story/f447a106a86b2735d6beb4ae1685c160.

[53]   M. Moore, "China abolishes its labour camps and releases prisoners," The Telegraph, 31 December 2018. [Online]. Available: https://www.telegraph.co.uk/news/worldnews/asia/china/10561434/China-abolishes-its-labour-camps-and-releases-prisoners.html.

[54]   T. Dharpo, "China deploys "hunter-killer" drones in high altitude border regions of Tibet, Xinjiang," Phayul, 7 December 2018. [Online]. Available: http://www.phayul.com/news/article.aspx?id=41007.

[55] W. contributors, "Nangpa La shooting incident," Wikipedia, The Free Encyclopedia., 12 June 2018. [Online]. Available: https://en.wikipedia.org/w/index.php?title=Nangpa_La_shooting_incident&oldid=845465917.

[56] W. contributors, "2014 Hong Kong protests," Wikipedia, The Free Encyclopedia., 28 December 2018. [Online]. Available: https://en.wikipedia.org/w/index.php?title=2014_Hong_Kong_protests&oldid=875779758.

[57] L. Kuo, "Chinese censors are trying to erase Hong Kong's pro-democracy movement," Quartz, 29 September 2014. [Online]. Available: https://qz.com/272690/chinese-censors-are-trying-to-erase-hong-kongs-pro-democracy-movement/.

[58] "Hong Kong pro-democracy politicians banned by China as crisis grows," The Guardian, [Online]. Available: https://www.theguardian.com/world/2016/nov/07/china-bans-hong-kong-pro-independence-politicians-crisis-grows.

[59] A. Wong, "As Hong Kong Chooses Its Next Leader, China Still Pulls the Strings," The New York Times, 23 March 2017. [Online]. Available: https://www.nytimes.com/2017/03/23/world/asia/hong-kong-chief-executive-ce-election-carrie-lam-john-tsang.html?_r=0.

[60] "Hong Kong court bans pro-independence politicians from office," The Guardian, [Online]. Available: https://www.theguardian.com/world/2016/nov/15/hong-kong-bans-pro-democracy-politicians-after-beijing-rewrites-oath-law.

[61] N. Levin, "Hong Kong Pro-Democracy Activist Joshua Wong Denied Entry to Thailand," The Wall Street Journal, 5 October 2016. [Online]. Available: https://www.wsj.com/articles/hong-kong-pro-democracy-activist-joshua-wong-detained-in-thailand-1475631648.

[62]   P. Popham, "Hong Kong protests: Demonstrators set for
        backlash as China's strangulation of the Umbrella Revolution
        begins," Independent, 5 October 2014. [Online]. Available:
        http://www.independent.co.uk/news/world/asia/hong-kong-
        protesters-set-for-backlash-as-chinas-strangulation-of-the-
        umbrella-revolution-begins-9774968.html.

[63]   "China tries to snuff out separatism in Hong Kong," The
        Economist, 12 November 2016. [Online]. Available:
        http://www.economist.com/news/china/21709801-it-will-do-
        little-curb-separatist-demands-china-intervenes-hong-kongs-
        oath-taking-row.

[64]   N. Vanderklippe, "Legislators challenging China's grip on
        Hong Kong barred from office," The Globe and Mail, 7
        November 2016. [Online]. Available:
        http://www.theglobeandmail.com/news/world/legislators-
        challenging-chinas-grip-on-hong-kong-barred-from-
        office/article32696075/.

[65]   N. Levin and N. Chaichalearmmongkol, "Hong Kong Pro-
        Democracy Activist Joshua Wong Denied Entry to Thailand,"
        The Wall Street Journal, 5 October 2016. [Online].
        Available: https://www.wsj.com/articles/hong-kong-pro-
        democracy-activist-joshua-wong-detained-in-thailand-
        1475631648.

[66]   L. Cochrane, "Deporting Hong Kong Umbrella Movement
        activist 'China's business', Thailand says," ABC News, 6
        October 2016. [Online]. Available:
        http://www.abc.net.au/news/2016-10-06/thailand-says-
        deporting-hong-kong-activist-was-chinas-business/7907192.

[67]   J. Siu, "Joshua Wong and other jailed Hong Kong student
        leaders see political careers halted," South China Morning
        Post, 17 August 2017. [Online]. Available:

http://www.scmp.com/news/hong-kong/politics/article/2107216/occupy-activists-joshua-wong-and-nathan-law-jailed-hong-kong.

[68] W. contributors, "Richard Gere," Wikipedia, The Free Encyclopedia., 10 January 2019. [Online]. Available: https://en.wikipedia.org/w/index.php?title=Richard_Gere&oldid=877753289.

[69] M. Oppenheim, "Richard Gere says he's been dropped from big Hollywood movies because China doesn't like him," Independent, 20 April 2017. [Online]. Available: http://www.independent.co.uk/arts-entertainment/films/news/richard-gere-big-hollywood-movies-China-tibet-buddhist-dalia-lama-chinese-audience-blockbusters-a7693256.html.

[70] W. contributors, "Anatomically modern human," Wikipedia, The Free Encyclopedia., 30 May 2015. [Online]. Available: https://en.wikipedia.org/w/index.php?title=Anatomically_modern_human&oldid=664775873.

[71] P. Thibodeau, "Obama: 'We don't have enough engineers'," ComputerWorld, 14 June 2011. [Online]. Available: https://www.computerworld.com/article/2508899/it-careers/obama—we-don-t-have-enough-engineers-.html.

[72] A. Gupta, "India: An innovation hub?," Fortune India, 2 May 2017. [Online]. Available: http://www.fortuneindia.com/technology/india-an-innovation-hub-/100207.

[73] "Remarks by Chairman Alan Greenspan," The Federal Reserve Board, 23 February 2004. [Online]. Available: https://www.federalreserve.gov/boarddocs/speeches/2004/20040223/.

[74] A. Singh, "Leverage 101: The Real Cause of the Financial Crisis," Seeking Alpha, 25 September 2008. [Online]. Available: https://seekingalpha.com/article/97299-leverage-101-the-real-cause-of-the-financial-crisis.

[75] W. contributors, "Normal distribution," Wikipedia, The Free Encyclopedia., 17 December 2018. [Online]. Available: https://en.wikipedia.org/w/index.php?title=Normal_distributio n&oldid=874223225.

[76] W. contributors, "Student's t-distribution," Wikipedia, The Free Encyclopedia., 3 December 2018. [Online]. Available: https://en.wikipedia.org/w/index.php?title=Student%27s_t-distribution&oldid=871839031.

[77] Financial Times, [Online]. Available: http://ftalphaville.ft.com/2009/06/24/58871/on-goldmans-fat-tail-risk/.

[78] R. Langreth, "The Oracle of Doom," Forbes, 15 January 2009. [Online]. Available: http://www.forbes.com/forbes/2009/0202/020.html.

[79] Financial Times, [Online]. Available: http://ftalphaville.ft.com/2009/01/22/51553/lord-turner-var-and-the-fsa/.

[80] T. Nath, "Fat Tail Risk: What It Means and Why You Should Be Aware Of It," Nasdaq, 2 November 2015. [Online]. Available: http://www.nasdaq.com/article/fat-tail-risk-what-it-means-and-why-you-should-be-aware-of-it-cm537614.

[81] M. Finke, "Can You Plan for a Black Swan?," ThinkAdvisor, 30 November 2015. [Online]. Available: http://www.thinkadvisor.com/2015/11/30/can-you-plan-for-a-black-swan.

[82]   W. contributors, "Long-Term Capital Management,"
        Wikipedia, The Free Encyclopedia., 2 November 2018.
        [Online]. Available:
        https://en.wikipedia.org/w/index.php?title=Long-
        Term_Capital_Management&oldid=866878483.

[83]   W. contributors, "National debt of the United States,"
        Wikipedia, The Free Encyclopedia., 4 January 2019.
        [Online]. Available:
        https://en.wikipedia.org/w/index.php?title=National_debt_of_
        the_United_States&oldid=876814599.

[84]   P. Garofalo, "Six Years After Cheney Said 'Deficits Don't
        Matter,' The National Debt Hits A 50-Year High,"
        ThinkProgress, 2 October 2008. [Online]. Available:
        http://thinkprogress.org/economy/2008/10/02/172396/cheney
        -deficit-debt/.

[85]   "Debt and Deficit Quotes," zFacts, [Online]. Available:
        http://zfacts.com/zfacts.com/p/467.html.

[86]   W. contributors, "Bretton Woods system," Wikipedia, The
        Free Encyclopedia., 23 December 2018. [Online]. Available:
        https://en.wikipedia.org/w/index.php?title=Bretton_Woods_s
        ystem&oldid=874997176.

[87]   S. Anthony, "Microsoft's share of the consumer market has
        dropped from 95% to 20% in 8 years," ExtremeTech, 13
        December 2012. [Online]. Available:
        https://www.extremetech.com/computing/143277-microsofts-
        share-of-the-consumer-market-has-dropped-from-95-to-20-in-
        8-years.

[88]   W. contributors, "United States v. Microsoft Corp.,"
        Wikipedia, The Free Encyclopedia., 29 December 2018.
        [Online]. Available:
        https://en.wikipedia.org/w/index.php?title=United_States_v._

Microsoft_Corp.&oldid=875919600.

[89]   W. contributors, "Globalization," Wikipedia, The Free
        Encyclopedia., 10 january 2019. [Online]. Available:
        https://en.wikipedia.org/w/index.php?title=Globalization&oldi
        d=877680736.

[90]   W. contributors, "Environmental issues in China," Wikipedia,
        The Free Encyclopedia., 9 January 2019. [Online]. Available:
        https://en.wikipedia.org/w/index.php?title=Environmental_iss
        ues_in_China&oldid=877517850.

[91]   D. Lague, "Corruption is linked to pollution in China - Asia -
        Pacific - International Herald Tribune," The New York
        Times, 21 August 2006. [Online]. Available:
        http://www.nytimes.com/2006/08/21/world/asia/21iht-
        smog.2550052.html.

[92]   N. Jenny, "Panama Papers lay bare China's corruption,
        environmental woes," Global Risk Insights, 15 April 2016.
        [Online]. Available:
        http://globalriskinsights.com/2016/04/panama-papers-china-
        corruption/.

[93]   L. Y. Ruan, "Why China Can't Fix Its Environment," The
        Dipolmat, 15 March 2015. [Online]. Available:
        http://thediplomat.com/2015/03/why-china-cant-fix-its-
        environment/.

[94]   G. D'Mello, "Workers At A Chinese Factory Are Shockingly
        Mistreated So You Can Have Your iPhone," Indiatimes, 17
        January 2018. [Online]. Available:
        http://www.indiatimes.com/technology/news/workers-at-a-
        chinese-factory-for-apple-are-severely-mistreated-so-you-can-
        have-your-iphone-337842.html.

[95] K. Doshi, "Land Acquisition in India: Is the farmer wrong...?,"
      Karan Doshi Self Publishing, [Online]. Available:
      http://www.amazon.in/Land-Acquisition-India-farmer-wrong-
      ebook/dp/B019ZH3Z1Y.

[96] M. Collins, "It is Time to Stand Up to China," IndustryWeek,
      13 June 2016. [Online]. Available:
      http://www.industryweek.com/trade/it-time-stand-china.

[97] U. C. Haley and G. T. Haley, "How Chinese Subsidies
      Changed the World," Harvard Business Review, 25 April
      2013. [Online]. Available: https://hbr.org/2013/04/how-
      chinese-subsidies-changed.

[98] U. C. V. Haley and G. T. Haley, "The Hidden Advantage of
      Chinese Subsidies," The World Financial Review, 14
      September 2014. [Online]. Available:
      http://www.worldfinancialreview.com/?p=2942.

[99] "WTO investigates allegations of illegal China subsidies," ABC
      News, [Online]. Available:
      http://abcnews.go.com/Business/story?id=3550476.

[100] M. L. Clifford, "Chinese Government Subsidies Play Major
      Part In Electric Car Maker BYD's Rise," Forbes, 26 July 2016.
      [Online]. Available:
      https://www.forbes.com/sites/mclifford/2016/07/26/with-a-
      little-help-from-its-friends-lavish-chinese-government-help-for-
      top-electric-car-maker-byd/#10b3dcc0115e.

[101] R. D. Atkinson, "The Explosive Rise of Subsidies to Chinese
      Industry," Information Technology and Innovative
      Foundation, 25 November 2013. [Online]. Available:
      https://itif.org/publications/2013/11/25/explosive-rise-
      subsidies-chinese-industry.

[102] "Perverse advantage," The Economist, 27 April 2013. [Online]. Available: https://www.economist.com/news/finance-and-economics/21576680-new-book-lays-out-scale-chinas-industrial-subsidies-perverse-advantage.

[103] D. McMahon, "Chinese Industrial Subsidies Grow 23%," The Wall Street Journal, 23 June 2013. [Online]. Available: https://www.wsj.com/articles/SB10001424127887323836504578551474072138676.

[104] "CHINA DEPLOYS STATE POWER TO DOMINATE GLOBAL STEEL INDUSTRY," Industry Today, [Online]. Available: https://industrytoday.com/article/china-deploys-state-power-to-dominate-global-steel-industry/.

[105] M. Collins, "It is Time to Stand Up to China," Industry Week, 13 June 2016. [Online]. Available: http://www.industryweek.com/trade/it-time-stand-china.

[106] W. contributors, "Sunway TaihuLight," Wikipedia, The Free Encyclopedia., 28 November 2018. [Online]. Available: https://en.wikipedia.org/w/index.php?title=Sunway_TaihuLight&oldid=871038893.

[107] W. contributors, "Chinese espionage in the United States," Wikipedia, The Free Encyclopedia., 21 December 2018. [Online]. Available: https://en.wikipedia.org/wiki/Chinese_espionage_in_the_United_States.

[108] S. Frizell, "Here's What Chinese Hackers Actually Stole From U.S. Companies," Time, 20 May 2014. [Online]. Available: http://time.com/106319/heres-what-chinese-hackers-actually-stole-from-u-s-companies/.

[109] "Chinese Hackers and America's "Revenge"," China Uncensored, 19 August 2015. [Online]. Available:

https://www.youtube.com/watch?v=XpVeZVNpHfg.

[110] J. Philipp, "CHINA SECURITY: China Reins in Its Hacker Army," The Epoch Times, 16 November 2015. [Online]. Available: https://www.theepochtimes.com/china-security-china-reins-in-its-hacker-army_1894442.html.

[111] J. Philipp, "EXCLUSIVE: How Hacking and Espionage Fuel China's Growth," The Epoch Times, 10 September 2015. [Online]. Available: http://www.theepochtimes.com/n3/1737917-investigative-report-china-theft-incorporated/.

[112] G. D'Mello, "China Allegedly Used This Tiny Chip You Can Barely See To Hack Into Apple, Amazon & US Govt PCs," Indiatimes, 5 October 2018. [Online]. Available: https://www.indiatimes.com/technology/news/china-allegedly-used-this-tiny-chip-you-can-barely-see-to-hack-into-apple-amazon-us-govt-pcs-354272.html.

[113] M. Hvistendahl, "China's theft of U.S. trade secrets under scrutiny," Science, 28 February 2017. [Online]. Available: http://www.sciencemag.org/news/2017/02/china-s-theft-us-trade-secrets-under-scrutiny.

[114] "A new approach to China," Google, 10 January 2010. [Online]. Available: https://googleblog.blogspot.in/2010/01/new-approach-to-china.html.

[115] J. Cook, "FBI Director: China Has Hacked Every Big US Company," Business Insider, 6 October 2014. [Online]. Available: https://www.businessinsider.in/FBI-Director-China-Has-Hacked-Every-Big-US-Company/articleshow/44497504.cms.

[116] R. Massey, "A £30,000 copycat Rolls-Royce? It must be made in China," The Daily Mail, 23 April 2009. [Online]. Available: http://www.dailymail.co.uk/news/article-1172635/A-30-000-copycat-Rolls-Royce-It-China.html.

[117] M. Tisshaw, "Jaguar Land Rover continues legal battle against LandWind X7 copycat," AutoCar UK, 4 June 2016. [Online]. Available: https://www.autocar.co.uk/car-news/guangzhou-motor-show/range-rover-evoque-versus-landwind-x7-copycat-which-better.

[118] B. Iyer, "Continued: 50 Copy cat cars from China," CarToq, 18 January 2017. [Online]. Available: http://www.cartoq.com/continued-50-copy-cat-cars-from-china.

[119] "These 32 Ridiculous Chinese Knockoffs Are So Bad... You Can't Help But Laugh," canyouactually.com, [Online]. Available: http://canyouactually.com/these-32-ridiculous-chinese-knockoffs-are-so-bad-you-cant-help-but-laugh/.

[120] J. Bergman, "Top 10 Chinese Knockoffs," Time, 22 June 2010. [Online]. Available: http://content.time.com/time/specials/packages/article/0,28804,1998580_1998579_1998574,00.html.

[121] C. J. Strusiewicz, "The 5 Most Insane Examples of Chinese Counterfeiting," Cracked, 19 March 2012. [Online]. Available: http://www.cracked.com/article_19742_the-5-most-insane-examples-chinese-counterfeiting.html.

[122] I. Luo, "7 Military Weapons China Copied From the United States," The Epoch Times, 21 October 2017. [Online]. Available: http://www.theepochtimes.com/n3/1699756-7-military-weapons-china-copied-from-the-united-states/.

[123] "China crisis," The Guardian, 22 August 1999. [Online]. Available:

https://www.theguardian.com/theobserver/1999/aug/22/life1.li femagazine2.

[124] J. Risen and J. Gerth, "China Stole Nuclear Secrets From Los Alamos, U.S. Officials Say," The New York Times, 6 March 1999. [Online]. Available: https://partners.nytimes.com/library/world/asia/030699china-nuke.html.

[125] M. Vadum, "FLASHBACK: BILL CLINTON GAVE CHINA MISSILE TECHNOLOGY," Frontpage Mag, 21 December 2016. [Online]. Available: http://www.frontpagemag.com/fpm/265200/flashback-bill-clinton-gave-china-missile-matthew-vadum.

[126] B. Franken and P. Thomas, "Report: Stolen data gives China advanced nuclear know-how," CNN, 24 May 1999. [Online]. Available: http://edition.cnn.com/US/9905/24/cox.report.02/.

[127] S. Frizell, "Here's What Chinese Hackers Actually Stole From U.S. Companies," Time, 20 May 2014. [Online]. Available: http://time.com/106319/heres-what-chinese-hackers-actually-stole-from-u-s-companies/.

[128] "Could China build Britain's Hinkley nuclear power plant using stolen US technology?," RT, 11 August 2016. [Online]. Available: https://www.rt.com/uk/355512-hinkley-china-espionage-nuclear/.

[129] "Chinese Missile Allegations: Key Stories," Washington Post, [Online]. Available: http://www.washingtonpost.com/wp-srv/politics/special/missile/keystories.htm.

[130] "HUGHES ACCUSED OF AIDING CHINA," Wired, 9 December 1998. [Online]. Available: https://www.wired.com/1998/12/hughes-accused-of-aiding-

china.

[131] "China's Military Built with Cloned Weapons," USNI News,
       27 October 2015. [Online]. Available:
       http://news.usni.org/2015/10/27/chinas-military-built-with-
       cloned-weapons.

[132] "Xi Jinping urges world to 'say no to protectionism'," The
       Hindu, 17 January 2017. [Online]. Available:
       https://www.thehindu.com/news/international/Xi-Jinping-
       urges-world-to-%E2%80%98say-no-to-
       protectionism%E2%80%99/article17050763.ece.

[133] W. contributors, "Modernization of the People's Liberation
       Army," Wikipedia, The Free Encyclopedia., 22 October
       2018. [Online]. Available:
       https://en.wikipedia.org/w/index.php?title=Modernization_of_
       the_People%27s_Liberation_Army&oldid=865180072.

[134] H. J. Kazianis, "The Chinese Military Report You Missed
       (But Need to Read, Now)," The National Interest, 8
       December 2015. [Online]. Available:
       http://nationalinterest.org/blog/the-buzz/the-chinese-military-
       report-you-missed-need-read-now-14545.

[135] "US put China-made parts in F-35 fighter program," CNBC, 3
       June 2014. [Online]. Available:
       http://www.cnbc.com/2014/01/03/us-put-china-made-parts-in-
       f-35-fighter-program.html.

[136] A. Panda, "US Firm Under Investigation For Using Made-in-
       China Parts in F-35 Components," The Diplomat, 15 January
       2014. [Online]. Available:
       http://thediplomat.com/2014/01/us-firm-under-investigation-
       for-using-made-in-china-parts-in-f-35-components/.

[137] W. contributors, "For Want of a Nail," Wikipedia, The Free Encyclopedia., 8 January 2019. [Online]. Available: https://en.wikipedia.org/w/index.php?title=For_Want_of_a_N ail&oldid=877407688.

[138] B. Evans, "North Korean parents 'eating their own children' after being driven mad by hunger in famine-hit pariah state," The Daily Mail, 13 January 2013. [Online]. Available: http://www.dailymail.co.uk/news/article-2269094/North-Korean-parents-eat-children-driven-mad-hunger-famine-hit-pariah-state.html.

[139] J. Wiessman, "How Kim Jong Il Starved North Korea," The Atlantic, 20 December 2011. [Online]. Available: https://www.theatlantic.com/business/archive/2011/12/how-kim-jong-il-starved-north-korea/250244/.

[140] H. Gavin, "Inside North Korea's gulags: The shocking conditions in Kim's political prison camps," Sunday Express, 14 November 2017. [Online]. Available: https://www.express.co.uk/news/world/878003/kim-jong-un-north-korea-brutal-reeducation-gulag-prison-camps-revealed.

[141] C. Kitching, "Ex-guard at North Korean concentration camp reveals horrific treatment of prisoners with some beheaded and babies buried alive," Mirror, 30 April 2017. [Online]. Available: https://www.mirror.co.uk/news/world-news/ex-guard-north-korean-concentration-10328731.

[142] J. McDonald, "Chinese company 'sold North Korea nuclear bomb materials'," Independent, 21 September 2016. [Online]. Available: http://www.independent.co.uk/news/business/news/china-north-korea-nuclear-bomb-company-investigation-a7320266.html.

[143] J. Warrick, "Kim Jong Un's rockets are getting an important boost — from China," The Washinghton Post, 13 April 2017. [Online]. Available: https://www.washingtonpost.com/world/national-security/kim-jong-uns-rockets-are-getting-an-important-boost--from-china/2017/04/12/4893b0be-1a43-11e7-bcc2-7d1a0973e7b2_story.html?utm_term=.53e083dd8f72.

[144] E. Cheng, "Five ways North Korea gets money to build nuclear weapons," CNBC, 18 April 2017. [Online]. Available: https://www.cnbc.com/2017/04/18/how-does-north-korea-get-money-to-build-nuclear-weapons.html.

[145] "How North Korea Got Its "Made in China" Nukes," Huffington Post, 13 April 2017. [Online]. Available: http://www.huffingtonpost.com/peter-navarro-and-greg-autry/how-north-korea-got-its-m_b_9676424.html.

[146] W. C. T. II, "Mileposts on the road to a North Korean missile," The Washington Times, 10 July 2017. [Online]. Available: http://www.washingtontimes.com/news/2017/jul/10/north-korean-missile-closer-to-reality-with-chines/.

[147] "China expected to give $6 billion in aid to Pakistan as PM Imran Khan meets President Xi Jinping: Report," The Economic Times, 2 November 2018. [Online]. Available: https://economictimes.indiatimes.com/news/international/world-news/china-expected-to-give-6-billion-in-aid-to-pak-as-pm-khan-meets-prez-xi-report/articleshow/66477346.cms.

[148] A. Kingsbury, "Why China Helped Countries Like Pakistan, North Korea Build Nuclear Bombs," U.S. News, 2 June 2009. [Online]. Available: http://www.usnews.com/news/world/articles/2009/01/02/why-china-helped-countries-like-pakistan-north-korea-build-

nuclear-bombs.

[149] W. Burr, "China, Pakistan, and the Bomb:," The National Security Archive, 5 March 2004. [Online]. Available: http://nsarchive.gwu.edu/NSAEBB/NSAEBB114.

[150] J. Norbu, "Who Created Pakistan's Nuclear Arsenal?," Huffington Post, 20 May 2011. [Online]. Available: http://www.huffingtonpost.com/jamyang-norbu/who-created-pakistans-nuc_b_864124.html?ir=India&adsSiteOverride=in.

[151] "China's Nuclear Warning," The Wall Street Journal, 23 April 2015. [Online]. Available: http://www.wsj.com/articles/chinas-nuclear-warning-1429831422.

[152] T. Weiner, "NUCLEAR ANXIETY: THE KNOW-HOW; U.S. and China Helped Pakistan Build Its Bomb," The New York Times, 1 June 1998. [Online]. Available: http://www.nytimes.com/1998/06/01/world/nuclear-anxiety-the-know-how-us-and-china-helped-pakistan-build-its-bomb.html.

[153] W. contributors, "2008 Mumbai attacks," Wikipedia, The Free Encyclopedia., 12 January 2019. [Online]. Available: https://en.wikipedia.org/w/index.php?title=2008_Mumbai_att acks&oldid=878018697.

[154] "China again sides with Pakistan, blocks UN move to ban Masood Azhar," The Economic Times, 12 July 2018. [Online]. Available: http://economictimes.indiatimes.com/news/defence/china-again-sides-with-pakistan-blocks-un-move-to-ban-masood-azhar/articleshow/56256016.cms.

[155] "Opposed to China's CPEC that passes through PoK, India boycotts Belt and Road initiative," India Today, 13 May 2017. [Online]. Available: http://indiatoday.intoday.in/story/one-

belt-one-road-pakistan-occupied-kashmir-china-cpec-
beijing/1/953313.html.

[156] K. Hunt, "China installs weapons on contested South China
Sea islands, report says," CNN, 15 December 2016. [Online].
Available: http://edition.cnn.com/2016/12/14/asia/south-
china-sea-artificial-islands-spratlys-weapon-systems/.

[157] "Chinese navy holds live-fire drills in South China Sea," New
Straits Times, 10 July 2016. [Online]. Available:
https://www.nst.com.my/news/2016/07/157430/chinese-navy-
holds-live-fire-drills-south-china-sea.

[158] M. Mogato, "Philippine officials say China blocked access to
disputed South China Sea atoll," Reuters, 29 January 2016.
[Online]. Available: http://www.reuters.com/article/us-
southchinasea-china-philippines-idUSKCN0W402A.

[159] D. Gayle, "Chinese ships ram Vietnamese vessels and fire
water cannon injuring sailors in maritime clash over new oil
rig that Hanoi says is in its territorial waters," The Daily Mail,
7 May 2014. [Online]. Available:
http://www.dailymail.co.uk/news/article-2622152/Vietnam-
tries-stop-China-oil-rig-deployment.html.

[160] A. Panda, "International Court Issues Unanimous Award in
Philippines v. China Case on South China Sea," The
Diplomat, 12 July 2016. [Online]. Available:
https://thediplomat.com/2016/07/international-court-issues-
unanimous-award-in-philippines-v-china-case-on-south-china-
sea/.

[161] "Thatcher and the Soviet Union: The Iron Lady who helped
bring down the 'Evil Empire'," RT, 9 April 2013. [Online].
Available: http://www.rt.com/op-edge/thatcher-ussr-cold-war-
gorbachev-528/.

[162] W. contributors, "Obesity in the Middle East and North Africa," Wikipedia, The Free Encyclopedia., 22 August 2018. [Online]. Available: https://en.wikipedia.org/w/index.php?title=Obesity_in_the_Middle_East_and_North_Africa&oldid=856034674.

[163] J. Lane, "Shale vs OPEC: What's going on with oil prices? Will the bleeding stop, and when?," BiofuelsDigest, 13 January 2015. [Online]. Available: http://www.biofuelsdigest.com/bdigest/2015/01/13/shale-vs-opec-whats-going-on-with-oil-prices-will-the-bleeding-stop-and-when.

[164] The IntMath blog, [Online]. Available: https://www.intmath.com/blog/wp-content/images/2008/02/co2-data-noaab.gif.

[165] P. Gwalani, "Resident enters Mumbai in Guinness World Records and Limca Book of Records for potholes," Mumbai Mirror, 22 July 2018. [Online]. Available: https://mumbaimirror.indiatimes.com/mumbai/civic/resident-enters-mumbai-in-guinness-for-potholes/articleshow/65086524.cms.

[166] J. Shankleman and H. Warren, "Solar Power Will Kill Coal Faster Than You Think," Bloomberg, 15 June 2017. [Online]. Available: https://www.bloomberg.com/news/articles/2017-06-15/solar-power-will-kill-coal-sooner-than-you-think.

[167] K. Chandrasekaran, "Solar power tariff drops to historic low at Rs 2.44 per unit," The Economic Times, 13 May 2017. [Online]. Available: https://economictimes.indiatimes.com/industry/energy/power/solar-power-tariff-drops-to-historic-low-at-rs-2-44-per-unit/articleshow/58649942.cms.

[168] S. Hanley, "Electric Car Myth Buster — Efficiency," Clean Technica, 10 March 2018. [Online]. Available: https://cleantechnica.com/2018/03/10/electric-car-myth-buster-efficiency/.

[169] "The Future of Airbus Airliners is Hybrid Electric - AINtv," Aviation International News, 15 July 2014. [Online]. Available: https://www.youtube.com/watch?v=71blB6hNV0g.

[170] W. contributors, "Electricity sector in India," Wikipedia, The Free Encyclopedia., 11 January 2019. [Online]. Available: https://en.wikipedia.org/w/index.php?title=Electricity_sector_in_India&oldid=877805563.

www.ingramcontent.com/pod-product-compliance
Lightning Source LLC
Chambersburg PA
CBHW031051250726

48655CB00004B/1392